MW00675238

SUPER-HUMAN PERFORMANCE

SUPER-HUMAN PERFORMANCE

UTILIZING YOUR GIFTS TO PERFORM AT EXTRAORDINARY LEVELS

DARRAYL & DERRICK MILES

MILESTONE
PUBLISHING HOUSE

Published by Milestone Publishing House

Unless otherwise noted, all Scripture quotations are from New King James Version.

Scripture quotations marked NIV are from the Holy Bible, New International Version. Copyright © 1973, 1978, 1984, International Bible Society. Used by permission. 1984

Scripture quotations marked ESV are from the Holy Bible, English Standard Version. Copyright © 2001 by Crossway Bibles, a division of Good News Publishers. Used by permission.

Scripture quotations marked NLT are from the Holy Bible, New Living Translation, copyright © 1996, 2004, 2007. Used by permission of Tyndale House Publishers, Inc., Wheaton, IL 60189. All rights reserved.

Scripture quotations marked KJV are from the King James Version of the Bible.

Cover design by Roy Roper
Interior design by Terry Clifton

Library of Congress Control Number: 2010913133

International Standard Book Number: 978-0-9828393-3-1
E-book ISBN: 978-0-9828393-9-3

First Edition

11 12 13 14 15 — 9 8 7 6 5 4 3 2 1
Printed in Canada

DEDICATION

This book is dedicated to the billions of people worldwide that have a unique Gift to complete their ultimate assignment on earth. It is our hope that this book series encourages us to learn our Gifts and strategically apply those Gifts to improve the lives of others.

Contents

The Gift of Giving in Action. ix

Acknowledgements xiii

Foreword   The Happiest Place on Earth is Working
in God's Magic Kingdom. xv

Introduction xix

Gift Preview xxix

Chapter 1   From Samson to Superhuman Servant 1

*Darrayl Miles: Discerning the Gifts in Others
to Achieve Superhuman Performance
Gift: Discernment*

Chapter 2   The Magic of Teamwork 9

*Pat Williams: Playing in the Arena of Life
Gift: Administration*

Chapter 3   Food for Thought 17

*Judson Allen: A Feast Fit for a King
Gift: Craftsmanship*

Chapter 4   When Business As Usual Won't Cut It!. 25

*Dave Kahle: Position Yourselves With Power
Gift: Writing*

Chapter 5   Listen to the Man in Your Corner. 35

*George Foreman: Knock Them Out With Love
Gift: Discernment*

Chapter 6   I'm Your Wake Up Call. 45

*Peter J. Daniels: Turn Back On Your Dream Machine
Gift: Administration*

Chapter 7   Ridiculous Faith 55

Shundrawn Thomas: Go in the Strength You Have
Gift: Faith

Chapter 8   Fishers of Men 65

Fred Fisher: Spending Your Time on People
Gift: Giving

Chapter 9   Today is a Great Day for a WOW! Image 71

Lavon Lewis: Your Image is Everything You Do
Gift: Craftsmanship

Chapter 10   "Play" It Forward................................79

Andre Hudson: Physically, Mentally & Spiritually Fit
Gift: Giving

Chapter 11   Growing Wealth God's Way 85

William R. Patterson: Making Your Pennies Prosper
Gift: Knowledge

Chapter 12   What's Your Story?.............................97

Eddie Jones: Writing to Make Your Joy Complete
Gift: Writing

Bonus Gift   Music...107

Bonus   Push Your Dreams as if They Were as Light
as a Feather 109

Abraham McDonald: From Obscurity to Oprah
Gift: Music

Appendix   Related Reading 117

Bibliography...121

The Milestone Brand 123

About the Authors.......................................125

THE GIFT OF GIVING IN ACTION

Darrayl and Derrick Miles are exercising their Gift of Giving by donating 10% of all proceeds of the Superhuman Performance® franchise to two of their favorite charities:

- Metro Hope For Kids Project
- Orlando Magic Youth Foundation

If you believe in helping our children reach their maximum potential; please consider a donation.

ORLANDO MAGIC YOUTH FOUNDATION
WHERE YOU MAKE THE DIFFERENCE.

ORLANDO MAGIC YOUTH FOUNDATION

There is no doubt that children—their dreams, their hopes and their potential—represent our future. From educational and arts programs to health programs focused on preventing childhood obesity, the Orlando Magic Youth Foundation is dedicated to nourishing the minds and bodies of children that need it most. Over the last 21 years, the OMYF has distributed more than $16 million to local non-profit community organizations.

The OMYF raises community dollars annually through donations, auctions and events such as the Black Tie and Tennies Gala and the OMYF Open Golf Tournament. With administrative costs covered, 100% of your gift goes directly to benefit children. Plus the McCormick Foundation provides a $.50 match to make your donation go even further!

Make your difference today by donating at **omyf.org**.

METRO HOPE FOR KIDS

Out of the pain, impoverishment and isolation of his own abandonment, Bill Wilson established Metro Ministries in 1980 in what was one of Brooklyn's roughest neighborhoods. Over the years, he has developed a heart of compassion for suffering children everywhere. From the ghettos of America to the townships of South Africa, villages of Eastern Europe, slums of India and islands of the Philippines, he has rescued hurting children and given them hope for the future. Every week 40,000 children in these countries are being touched with love.

With a mandate to help, I'm looking for ordinary people with extraordinary hearts who are willing to give of their time, talents and finances. I need your help to change an old, condemned hospital in Brooklyn, NY, into a community food-and-clothing pantry, as well as a place to hold after-school programs for boys and girls, mentoring programs for youth, and adult programs to help men and women who are coming out of drug addiction. Will you say yes and join a team that makes a difference?

For more information or to give to Metro Hope For Kids, go to www.metrohopeforkids.org. Your donations will change possibilities into realities for boys and girls around the world. Thank you for being one who makes a difference in the life of a child!

—ROSELLA ANGEL RIDINGS,
  Founder

ACKNOWLEDGEMENTS

We would like to thank every individual that took the time to be interviewed on our radio program Superhuman Performance®. Your willingness to be a blessing to others ultimately lead to the advent of the Superhuman Performance franchise. We promise to continue to use our time and talents to create tools and services that improve the lives of billions of people around the world:

Roger Andersen	Ken Blanchard	Darren Hardy
Jay Lowder	Joel Wiggins	Pastor Sunday Adelaja
Genma Stringer Holmes	Darrayl Miles	Frederick E. Fisher
Abraham McDonald	Elayna Fernandez	Buck Jacobs
Ricc Rollins	Paul Kennedy	Barry Eggleston
Chad Revelle	Dr. Mark Chironna	Os Hillman
Darlene McCoy	Shundrawn Thomas	Pam Perry
Larry Julian	Pat Williams	Angela Johnson McGee
George Fraser	Elmer Towns	H. Daniel Wilson
Chef Judson Todd Allen	Mitchell Silver	Alma Rivera
Angella Kenyatta	Kamille Wright	Paul Cuny
Eddie Jones	Teri Werner	Tom Blackaby
Jerry Moll	Suzie Belforado	Apostle Ron Spears
Dr. Caroline Leaf	Wess Morgan	Keith Harrell
Ed Houston	Amy Fisher	Mike Rover
Pam Boney	Steve Marr	Patrice Tsague
Jill Stanton Bullard	Evelyn Neely	Derrick Miles

Nikki D. Washington
Chandra Sparks Taylor
Marguerite Evans
Pastor Kelvin McCree
Adrian Freeman
Eligious Taderera
Tanya Dallas Lewis
Dave Kahle
Wende Jones
Apostle John Kelly
Korey Bowie
Kevin Harrington
Marjane
Andy Albright
Don Barefoot
Alton Jamison
Todd Dulaney
Lloyd Reeb
Derwin Gray

Yvonne Brown
William R. Patterson
Chris Davis
Timothy McCann
Melissa Giovagnoli
Jin Stu Robertson
Rufus Curry Jr.
Everett Glenn
Kelvin Redd
Pastor Jonathan Leath
Phyllis Caddell M
Shawn Harper
David Riklan
Kim Person
Gary Johnson
Monica Davis
Ami Rushes
LeCrae
Krista Dunk

Don Dewberry
Cory George
George Foreman
Al Reynolds
Carol Mackey
Dr. Michael Woody
Pastor Miles McPherson
Peter J. Daniels
Bishop Emmanuel Jatau
Lisa McClendon
Dr. Kenneth Whalum
Canton Jones
LaVon Lewis
Bryan Caraway
D. Keith Pigues
Cheneta Jones
Maurice Brailsford
Michael V. Roberts
Gilbert Esquivel

THE HAPPIEST PLACE ON EARTH IS WORKING IN GOD'S MAGIC KINGDOM

And it shall come to pass afterward, that I will pour out
my spirit upon all flesh; and your sons and your daughters
shall prophesy, your old men shall dream dreams, your
young men shall see visions.

—JOEL 2:28 ,KJV

Arthur watched his friend's eyes grow wide with excitement as
the car turned off the main highway and onto a dusty drive,
bouncing over rutted rows carved out by farm equipment and
trucks. To the east, he saw the snow-capped slopes of the San
Bernardino Mountains, the range shimmering silver as the long
rays of dusk broke through the clouds. To the west, a copper sun
sank slowly into the Pacific Ocean. Beyond the hood of the car
lay 160 acres of dirt where bulldozers had cleared orange groves.
The year was 1954, and Arthur sat anxiously in the passenger's
seat. An hour south of Los Angeles and already he was tired of
the vast wasteland. He could smell the acrid odor of his perspi-
ration soaking through his shirt. The trip was a mistake and his

friend Walter, a wild man. Who in his right mind would buy land down here and build anything except an equipment shed?

The car stopped. Arthur's friend pointed straight ahead. "Right over there. Where the trees end. That'll be yours."

"It's a big field of dirt clods, Walt."

"Of course. It's a field. That's why it's cheap."

"Three million dollars isn't cheap," Arthur said.

"I'd buy it myself," Walt said, "but I'm all tapped out. Couldn't even afford to buy this piece, to be honest with you. Brother had a fit when I told him to make the down payment. It'll be worth millions, someday, though. You'll see. So will yours."

"I don't know. That's a lot of money for acres and acres of dirt."

"You're not buying dirt, Arthur. You're buying a dream. There's a fortune to be made here. If you buy up all the property around mine, in a year or two, it'll be worth twenty times what you paid for it."

"Tell me again how this park of yours is going to work. Maybe I missed something."

Walt turned off the engine and stepped out. Arthur followed, wishing, now, he'd kept his mouth shut.

"It's not going to be just any park," Walt said. "It'll be magical."

"Right. An enchanted amusement park."

"Think of it more as a kingdom. It'll have a castle and moat with guards, wizards, princes, and princesses, trains, lagoons, and futuristic spaceship rides. You'll see."

"You got a name for this park?" Arthur said.

"Mouse Park."

"You're kidding, right? Who's going to pay to come play in a mouse park?"

"Okay, we'll work on the name. The point is, this'll be a place where dreams come true. I got the plans all right here, in my head. There'll be a big outdoor bandstand over there, and near where the car, is we're going to have a village with a town hall, fire and police stations, restaurants, and shops. The whole works."

"Why not put your tiny town in that clearing?" Arthur asked, pointing toward a wide swath of tumbleweeds and sagebrush. "That way, you wouldn't have to knock down as many trees."

"My Wild West settlement goes on that plot."

"I suppose you'll have cowboys and horses and gun fighters."

"Wouldn't be much of a frontier village without those, would it? Plus, we'll have stagecoach rides, a saloon with a theater inside, can-can girls, the whole bit."

"I wish I had your vision, Walt. I really do."

"You can. You just have to believe."

"Here's what I believe: I believe I'll pass on this wonderful opportunity of yours and stick with show business. At least that's a sort of make-believe foolishness I understand."

The next year, Disneyland opened with eighteen attractions, including the Jungle Cruise, Tomorrowland, Autopia, Mr. Toad's Wild Ride, and Mark Twain Riverboat Ride. Ronald Reagan, Bob Cummings, and Walt's good friend Arthur Linkletter—the one who'd passed up the chance to make millions—hosted the televised grand opening.

Years later, Arthur would reflect on his first trip to what had become Disneyland and say, "I didn't want to spoil Walt's enthusiasm, but after we had driven nearly an hour south of L.A., into the country, I thought, *My poor, delusional friend. You're going to put a bunch of merry-go-rounds and roller-coasters out here, forty-five minutes from Los Angeles. You'll go broke!*"

"A few years later," Arthur added, "I was at a birthday party at my friend's home. Walt pulled me aside and said, 'Art, I want your opinion on something. I can get 10,000 acres in Florida, enough land to do all the things I've dreamed of. I can build another Disneyland and have plenty of room for future projects. What do you think?' I told him, 'Walt, when you first told me you were going to build Disneyland, I thought it was a terrible idea. Well, I was wrong. But now, I think I've got some good advice for you: Don't build another Disneyland in Florida.' When he asked me why, I told him 'What you've got over in Anaheim is a one of a kind thing. Leave it that way.'"

But Walt Disney wasn't the sort of man to let a dream die. Are you?

> For I know the plans I have for you, declares the LORD, plans to prosper you and not to harm you, plans to give you hope and a future.
>
> —JEREMIAH 29:11, NIV

DESIGNED FOR SUCCESS

What would you do if you knew you wouldn't fail? What work, adventure, or great vision would you pursue if you knew, beyond a doubt, that you'd been called and gifted to succeed in that task? If you haven't done so already, I encourage you to carefully consider these questions. The answers will start you on the path to success that God has designed for you.

God blessed Walt Disney with the gifts of dreams, vision, and imagination. Even after he was fired by the *Kansas City Star* newspaper for his "lack of creativity," Walt knew he was born for something grand. And despite the ridicule of friends and employers, Walt persevered, pursuing the dream God placed within him.

Every day, men and women pave over the treasures buried deep within their hearts. They hear the call within and decide the voice is that of a wild man or woman, lost in a fit of abandon. "Quiet," they whisper. "I'm trying to work."

Ah, work. That thing many people do out of duty, not desire. What if you knew that God had placed within you gifts and dreams that were destined to give you hope, prosperity, and protection? Would you dig deep to find them? Your gifts, those natural talents and pent up passions that make you unique are God's seeds for success. They give power to your plans, purpose to your work, and pleasure to those around you. When you embrace your gifts, you follow in the footsteps of giants, men and women who have, over the years, changed cultures, liberated nations, and freed those in bondage.

> "I have a dream."
>
> —Dr. Martin Luther King Jr.
> The voice of man blessed with
> the gift of encouragement.

> "Mr. Gorbachev, tear down this wall!"
>
> —President Ronald Reagan
> The voice of man blessed with the gifts
> of leadership and administration.

> "If you can't feed a hundred people, then feed just one."
>
> —Mother Teresa of Calcutta
> The voice of a woman blessed with
> the gifts of faith and compassion.

> The kingdom of heaven is like treasure hidden in a field.
> When a man found it, he hid it again, and then in his joy
> went and sold all he had and bought that field.
>
> —Matthew 13:44, niv

Today you have an opportunity to change your life and the lives of others around you. People rarely achieve their greatest potential by waiting for life to begin. I've learned through years of leadership coaching that success, hope, and self-confidence flow from within as people utilize their natural gifts. Those who ignore their gifts often become discouraged, depressed, and defeated. This sense of frustration and failure rarely has anything to do with a person's talent, experience, or education. Rather, it results from a despondent spirit, a soul whose gifts remain buried and underutilized.

When people discover their gifts and put them to work, they develop deeper relationships, improve their lives, and change communities on a global level. Many of the world's most powerful leaders and influential personalities are using their talents to make the world a better place. By discovering your core leadership strengths, you too can serve others and give aid in a powerful way.

This book is a field manual, a guide for discovering your gifts, destiny, and the abundant joy God desires for you. Note, I didn't say happiness. Happiness depends on happenings, those circumstances that bring temporary delight. Joy comes when you use your God-given gifts for the good of those around you.

> God has given each of you a gift from his great variety of spiritual gifts. Use them well to serve one another.
> —1 Peter 4:10, NLT

What is a gift? How do you find your gifts? Is there a difference between natural talents and gifts? Over the course of your journey through this book, you'll explore a list of spiritual gifts and examine how they're manifested.

Perhaps once, long ago, you dreamed of something more than the mediocrity of a steady paycheck. If so, I invite you to take captive those secret longings and lay them before God. Your dreams, these divine desires, often point to your destiny and the discovery of your gifts.

Duty will not deliver you to the success you seek. It will only dull your senses and dampen your enthusiasm for the purpose to which you were called. In order to claim your gift, you must dig deep and find the treasure that lies buried in your heart. Christ calls you to come alive, so begin there, and ask yourself, "What stirs my heart? What moves me so much that I'm willing to do it even if there is no promise of reward?" Find that and you move into the realm of worship. You move into Superhuman Performance.

BORED, BURNED OUT & BUILT FOR SOMETHING BETTER

Everyone has a gift, a special ability that allows them to tap into Superhuman Performance. When you use your spiritual gifts, live with passion, and work with purpose, you honor God and receive His blessing. God said through the prophet Samuel, "Those who honor me, I will honor." (I Samuel 2:30, NIV) Isn't that what you want? To know your life matters, that your work will endure? Deep in your soul you know there's more to life than long commutes to a job. You sense God created you for good works, great adventures, and a lasting legacy. (Ephesians 2:10, NIV) So why is it so hard for some people to break free of the bonds that hold them down?

A recent Gallup Poll report revealed that most adults are dissatisfied with their jobs, even though it consumes the majority of their waking hours. They feel overly busy and stressed out. They buckle under the pressure of mounting financial debt. They worry about the future of their children, and yet less than one out of every 10 families pray together, study the Bible, or participate in regular expressions of faith. No wonder many people are bored, burned out, and burdened by worry. Some have lost touch of gifts God has given to them. And worse, others haven't discovered them. Could it be that they prefer the chains of contentment to a life of liberty and adventure?

I know for me, fear is exactly the thing that held me back. When I decided to launch The Milestone Brand, my wife worried that our lifestyle would suffer. She knew about my spiritual gifts; she'd seen how God had manifested Himself through me as I encouraged others. What scared her, though, was the fear that our income would suffer. But you know what? Our spiritual gifts and God's goodness aren't limited to a building, corporation, or career. His gifts are everlasting, and His word is rock solid. I'm convinced that where He leads, He feeds. Knowing you're destined for super-human success is one thing. To act on that knowledge and ask God to reveal your gifts takes faith.

I went into pre-medicine because I thought there was a lot of money in being a doctor. I found out later there's more money to be made in business than medicine. But at the time, medicine was my route to success. Then one day a couple students approached me while I was walking across the courtyard. One of them asked if I had ever thought about running for Junior Student Body President. I had to admit, that was the last thing on my mind. But a small voice told me to pay attention. I thought about it some more and finally added my name to the ballot.

Two weeks later, I won. That's when I learned an important lesson about discovering spiritual gifts. What others notice in us and say about us may be God's voice calling to us.

> Now to each one the manifestation of the Spirit is given for
> the common good.
> —I CORINTHIANS 12:7, NIV

After that election, I learned that I enjoyed leading others. People would tell me I had a gift, that I was a natural leader. But I also enjoyed medicine, and I didn't want to abandon that dream. Then I read a magazine article about Kevin Lofton, current president and CEO of Catholic Health Initiatives. I admired him for both his work in the field of medicine and his leadership skills. At the time of the article, he was the CEO of University of Alabama at Birmingham Hospital, a place I'd always wanted to work. A few weeks later, out of the blue, he called to ask me if I'd come to work for him. That's when I discovered the second important lesson about God's gifting. That is, once you start exercising your gifts, He opens doors.

WHAT IS A SPIRITUAL GIFT?

Spiritual gifts are supernatural endowments and abilities given to individuals for the good of God's people. Spiritual gifts are divine gratuities granted to Christ's followers. They are not natural abilities, though instinctive talents are part of God's grace, too. Everyone has certain innate skills, those exceptional qualities that, even without practice, allow them to excel with apparent ease.

Perhaps you knew a girl in high school who made straight As without cracking a book. Or you knew a boy who, with no formal musical training, played the piano by ear. Maybe you secretly resented that they mastered such complicated tasks with ease while you struggled. Raw talent can, in its natural form, invite envy, scorn, and jealousy.

Darrayl knows a kid named Omar who's about 16 years old. He fixes his sinks, lawn mower, electrical outlets, you name it. When you ask Omar how he knows how to do those things at such a young age, he replies, "I just tinker around with stuff until I fix them." My brother Darrayl can create a mean spreadsheet. Crunching numbers and solving formulas, that's his natural talent. The point is, he and Omar are both gifted in certain areas, but being mechanically or mathematically inclined aren't spiritual gifts. They're just God-given abilities.

SPIRITUAL GIFTS CARRY GREAT RESPONSIBILITY

Spiritual gifts are to be used for the good of others. In one sense, natural talent is a self-centered blessing. Gifted runners, math whizzes, or singers with perfect pitch may use their talents to bring glory and riches to themselves.

Spiritual gifts, on the other hand, are not to be used for personal gain, acquiring wealth, or amassing power. According to 1 Peter 4:10, people are to use their gifts to serve others and build up the Body of Christ. God graced the church of Corinth with every available gift. The Apostle Paul reminded them that they were "not lacking in any gift," and yet they suffered from divisions and quarrels. "I gave you milk, not solid food, for you were not ready for it. Indeed, you still are not ready. You are still worldly." As a community, the church of Corinth was more interested in boasting about its spiritual powers and who it followed than in serving one another.

Most Christians have two or three gifts in which they operate fluently. Some may have four, five, or six. But no one has all the gifts. God's goal is to bring people together, not divide them, so he makes everyone dependent on each other. You may wish for more gifts or different gifts, but God's will demands that people submit to one another as necessary.

My brother has the gift of discernment, so I always go to him when I need to make important decisions. I embrace his gift. The good news is that everyone has some spiritual gift. Jesus said, 'You will receive power when the Holy Spirit comes on you.' So if you're a new person in Christ, then you've received special power and at least one spiritual gift.

DISCOVERING YOUR SPIRITUAL GIFT

The Barna Group reports that nearly two-thirds of self-identified Christians say they've heard about spiritual gifts but can't accurately describe what a spiritual gift is. Of that group, 15 percent of people say they don't know their gift, 28 percent claim they don't have a gift, and 20 percent identify talents or skills, which don't qualify as spiritual gifts at all.

It's interesting what people consider spiritual gifts. I've seen people list good health, long life, happiness, patience and having a job, house, and sense of humor as spiritual gifts. Barna concluded that if more believers understood the nature and potential of God's special empowerment, the Christian church could radically impact the world in a positive way.

So how do you discover your spiritual gift? First, you have to be in God's word. If you can't name the gifts then you probably won't recognize them in yourself. In order to discover your gift, you'll need to ask God to reveal your gifts to you through the Spirit. By examining Scripture and observing how people in the Bible used their gifts, you can map your tendencies and see how your gifts are expressed.

Our giftedness is often a natural appreciation of certain kinds of ministry. Gifted people who serve successfully and impact others often attract people with similar gifts. That's what happened to me when I saw Colin Powell and Richard Parsons on TV. Something shook my spirit. I thought, *Man, I got to get to work.* I began to read all I could about leadership. I went back to school to obtain two masters degree because I was motivated from the inside. When you see others who have the same gift as you, something happens inside. You get excited. I'd say, any time that happens, pay attention.

Your gifts are woven into the fabric of who you are, so ask yourself, "What am I passionate about?" Chances are, your passions point to your gifts. Your greatest enemy is not a terrorist with a bomb or a collapsing economy. Your greatest threat is a life not lived. God has made you special for a particular purpose. Your job is to discover the field in which you're gifted and plow it. What would your life look like if you were doing what you wanted to do? Again, answer that question, and you'll begin to walk down the path that leads to superhuman success.

In this book, you'll explore seven spiritual gifts to see how Superhuman Performance is tied to God who loves you. As you read about Administration, Craftsmanship, Discernment, Faith, Giving, Knowledge, and Writing, consider if you possess one or more of these gifts. Then, when you're ready, you can move on to *Superhuman Performance II* and discover seven more gifts: Compassion, Encouragement, Helps/Serving, Hospitality, Leadership, Teaching, and Wisdom.

My prayer is that God will open your heart to the moving of His spirit, that He'll give you wisdom, discernment, and a passion for finding the life He desires for you. Thank you for allowing me to guide you on this exciting quest to find your spiritual gifts. Now let's turn the soil of your heart and begin to dig.

Superhumanly yours,

DERRICK MILES
"The Encourager"

Gift Preview

ADMINISTRATION

Administration is the gift God gives to some Christians that allows them to understand an organization's function and execute procedures that accomplish the goals of the ministry. This gift drives people to accomplish God-given goals and follow His directives by planning, organizing, and supervising other people.

People with this gift:

- Develop strategies or plans to reach identified goals.
- Assist ministries to become more effective and efficient.
- Create order out of organizational chaos.
- Act as managers or coordinators.
- Organize people, tasks, or events.

CRAFTSMANSHIP

Craftsmanship is the gift that gives some Christians the skill to create art in various forms so other people may experience spiritual responses of strength and inspiration. Through craftsmanship, the believer can build, maintain, or repair items used within the church.

People with this gift:

- Work with wood, cloth, paint, metal, glass, and other raw materials.

- Make things that increase the effectiveness of other people's ministries.

- Design and build tangible items and resources for ministry use.

- Work with different kinds of tools and are skilled with their hands.

- Use the arts to communicate God's truth.

- Develop and use artistic skills such as drama, art, music, and dance.

- Use variety and creativity to captivate people and cause them to consider Christ's message.

- Challenge people's perspective about God by using various forms of the arts.

- Demonstrate fresh ways to express the Lord's ministry and message.

DISCERNMENT

Discernment is the gift God gives to some Christians that allows them to know with assurance whether certain behavior or teaching is from God, Satan, human error, or human power. This gift helps people distinguish between truth and error, to discern the spirits, and to differentiate between good and evil, right and wrong.

People with this gift:

- Distinguish truth from error, right from wrong, pure motives from impure.

- Identify deception in others with accuracy and appropriateness.

- Determine whether a word attributed to God is authentic.

- Recognize inconsistencies in a teaching, prophetic message, or interpretation.

- Are able to sense the presence of evil.

FAITH

Faith is the gift God gives to some Christians that allows them to be firmly convinced of God's power, promises, and purpose. People with this gift display such a confidence in Him and His word that circumstances and obstacles do not shake their conviction.

People with this gift:

- Believe God's promises and inspire others to do the same.

- Act in complete confidence of God's ability to help them overcome obstacles.

- Demonstrate an attitude of trust in God's will and His promises.

- Advance Christ's cause because they go forward when others will not.

- Ask God for what is needed and trust Him for His provision.

GIVING

Giving is the gift that enables believers to recognize God's blessings and to respond to those blessings by generously, sacrificially, and cheerfully giving their resources (e.g., time, talent, or money) without thought of receiving something in return. People with this gift do not ask, "How much money do I need to give to God?" Instead, they ask "How much money do I need to live on?"

People with this gift:

- Meet tangible needs that enable spiritual growth to occur.

- Provide resources, generously and cheerfully, trusting God for His provision.

- May have a special ability to make money so that they may use it to further God's work.

KNOWLEDGE

Knowledge is the special gift whereby the Spirit enables certain people to understand in an exceptional way the great truths of God's word and to make them relevant to specific situations in the church. A person with this gift learns as much as possible through gathering much information and analyzing that data.

People with this gift:

- Receive truth which enables them to better serve others.

- Search the scriptures for insight, understanding, and truth.

- Gain knowledge which at times is not attained by natural means.

- Have an unusual insight or understanding that serves the church.

- Organize information for teaching and practical use.

WRITING

Writing is the gift that gives a believer the ability to express truth in written form, a form that can edify, instruct, and strengthen the community of believers.

People with this gift:

- Are better at expressing their thoughts in written form than in verbal form.

- Use writing to express other gifts.

- Write stories, sermons, devotions, histories, prayers, songs, or poetry to promote the body of Christ.

- Write based on inspiration from the Holy Spirit.

- Teach God's word to others through what they write.

CHAPTER 1

FROM SAMSON TO SUPERHUMAN SERVANT

Darrayl Miles: Discerning the Gifts in Others to Achieve Superhuman Performance

The tongue can bring death or life; those who love to talk will reap the consequences.

—PROVERBS 18:21, NLT

Name: Darrayl Miles
Position: Senior Vice President
Company: The Milestone Brand
Gift: Discernment

And be not conformed to this world: but be ye transformed by the renewing of your mind, that ye may prove what is that good, and acceptable, and perfect, will of God.

—ROMANS 12:2, KJV

From an early age, Darrayl Miles learned he could, with little effort, accomplish almost anything to which he put his mind.

2 / SUPERHUMAN PERFORMANCE

While others struggled with homework, Darrayl dallied, often waiting until the last minute to complete assignments. When he received his grades, however, they confirmed what he already knew: he could procrastinate and pass, and for a time that was good enough for Darrayl. He also learned he had the gift of persuasion.

"It didn't matter if it was my family, a football coach, or a Sunday school teacher,"

Darrayl says. "The group would always appoint me as their leader because they knew I could convince others to say 'Yes.' I was their point guy, and I made it a point to take care of my friends and me."

As a result of Darrayl's inflated opinion of himself, his ego expanded. "In short, I got the big head. When I was accepted into the college of my choice, I wasn't surprised. I expected it. I pledged a fraternity; they welcomed me enthusiastically. If there was an internship or job I wanted, it was mine. There wasn't anything I couldn't get. I was charismatic. I was also unruly, selfish, and obnoxious. I was a modern day Samson."

Darrayl didn't have the physical stature of Samson, but he did have power in a persuasive tongue. Samson was a man of great strength and an impressive leader. He had a tremendous anointing.

"He was also moody," explains Darrayl. "He was unpredictable, full of pride, and sexually immoral. When 30 men embarrassed him at his wedding, he killed them. Later he bludgeoned 1,000 men with a jawbone of a donkey. Yet with all this strength, ability, and anointing, Samson was easily defeated because of an unreachable spirit.

"I was like that. But instead of physically mutilating people, I killed them with words. Like Samson, when I was embarrassed and my pride wounded, I would lash out, deliberately tearing down that person. I would shatter their dream, kill their spirit, and leave them broken. I used my strength of speech to enact revenge. Because I misused my gift, I suffered the consequence. I didn't have many close friends because the perception was that I was a mean person; and I was. I was unreachable, unteachable, and intolerable."

THE TRANSFORMATION

Darrayl attended Florida A&M University, majoring in Biology. His goal was to become an optometrist. While in college, though, he found himself surrounded by other highly intelligent men and women, students who helped him see the flaws in his character and expose the pride that pushed so many away.

"I saw my tribe of friends working together to help each other get better. They held each other accountable for getting the best grades, for going beyond what was expected in the classroom. I'd been so accustomed to only doing enough to get by that their examples convicted me. They read books outside of the normal required reading list. I couldn't believe it! I did none of that. Worse, I had no mentor, no accountability partner, and no desire to be the best I could be."

One day, Darrayl had a conversation with his friend Shundrawn Thomas who happened to point out to him that there was no *i* in team.

"It's cliché today, but back then I thought, *How can this college kid have so much wisdom?* His words had a profound impact on me. But because of my pride, I refused to acknowledge how much that one comment changed my life. Shundrawn was exposed to the same college temptations the rest of us were facing, but his moral character never wavered. Not only did he have intellect and wisdom but he had a deep sense of spirituality. Later, I found out he was a preacher's kid."

Darrayl's second moment of transformation came when the manager of an optometry store suggested that Darrayl would make an excellent salesman. "You're articulate, good with customers, and have a lot of energy," his manager told him.

"Without hesitating, I jumped at the chance to go into sales. The idea that I could make that kind of money in college blew me away. And my manager was right. I was extremely good at sales! From that point, my life changed. I went from struggling college student putting $1.50 in the gas tank to get to class to college student who finally had enough money to buy suits. And not just one suit but lots of them. At the same time, I realized I needed a mentor, someone to guide me. I began reading books outside of class and just had this sense that I needed a tribe of friends to hold me accountable. All of that came, I think, from reflecting on what Shundrawn had said about needing a team. I began reading about successful people, subscribing to *Success* magazine, calling people I admired, asking them to mentor me. I prepared like never before in order to get the best grades I could."

PREPARATION

Because he became more aware of his talents, Darrayl's propensity to procrastinate vanished. "I began to actively change my work ethic. I remember reading in *Success* magazine an article about a young African American business owner who was performing at an extremely high level. He attributed his success to reading a book titled *The Power of Positive Thinking*. He mentioned that he too used to procrastinate, but that book encouraged him to show up for everything—work, class, and life—in a mighty way. He said the book helped him believe in himself, stop fuming and fretting, break the worry habit, and begin to solve problems. I bought it!"

Armed with the right tools, Darrayl broke the undisciplined spirit and prepared himself for the workforce. "I entered the job market with the realization that all companies had problems, and they hired people to solve those problems. Needless to say, I moved pretty fast through the junior ranks and quickly got a bump in salary and position. I started in sales and was quickly promoted to product manager. When I saw how much the outside sales reps made, I moved into outside sales. Each step along the way, I took what I'd learned from the previous experience and applied it at the next level.

"I was in my element as an outside salesman. I could manage my own schedule, use my gift of persuasion, and avoid being trapped up in an office. The other thing about outside sales was that I could run a multimillion dollar business with no investment of my own. I could market and allocate resources, track trends, and act on them—all with the company's money.

"But the farther I moved up the ladder, the more I came to realize I couldn't get others to follow. I had the skills and knowl-edge, but I lacked the compassion and character to lead a team. It was that old pride thing again, showing up in proportion to my success. My words to others were sharp and cut to the core. Who wanted to follow that?

"Fortunately, while I was working for Colgate Palmolive I had a manager, Bill Kroll, who exhibited caring, patience, and trust. I worked hard for him because he proved that he cared not only about my performance and career but also about me. He was the one who demonstrated to me what true leadership looked like. As a result, today I run a very successful insurance agency."

REVELATION

> And whatsoever ye do, do it heartily, as to the Lord, and
> not unto men.
>
> —COLOSSIANS 3:23, KJV

In the spring of 2009, Darrayl's brother, Derrick, shared with him his vision for teaching others about the need to examine their spiritual gifting. The idea intrigued Darrayl and filled a void he felt in his own spirit.

"After my brother came to me with the idea of working within the realm of my spiritual gifting, I began to study what it means to have an anointing of God's spirit and be given gifts for that purpose. As we researched our ministry, we came across a report from the Barna Group that showed only 21 percent of Christians had heard of a spiritual gift, and most couldn't name one. Many considered a sense of humor, being well-liked, drawing, and just going to church as spiritual gifts. Barna concluded that if more believers understood the nature and potential of Gods special empowerment, the global impact of the Christian body would be multiplied substantially.

"I took the spiritual gift assessment and found that I had gifts of discernment, encouragement, and faith. I wasn't surprised. I'd been using these gifts for years, though not necessarily for the good of others. I hadn't been speaking words of encouragement to lift up. I hadn't been discerning the heart of someone in order to challenge them to become better. Once I understood the gravity of using my gift for good, not for profit, I began to see how God brought others into my life so I could bless them through my gifts.

> The day soldiers stop bringing you their problems is the
> day you have stopped leading them.
> —GENERAL COLIN POWELL

"Today, I seek out business opportunities that are closest aligned with my gifts. I've moved from a life that was largely undefined to a life of purpose, from a life that lacked direction to one shaped by His design."

FITTED OUT FOR HIS WORK

If you are to serve God with all your heart, you will need to know what makes your heart race, what makes your spirit soar. When Paul commanded the church in Colossians to serve God whole heartedly, he meant in all things, even the mundane matters. But we all know it's easier to give your heart to a task when you are passionate about the activity and believe your calling has a purpose.

"It really doesn't matter how much money you make." "If you're not happy in your purpose, if you're not putting God's gifts and talents to work, then you'll experience a great deal of uneasiness in your life. I'd venture to say most people have no idea that their gifting is buried inside. They're working at a job they hate because they're fitted out for another purpose but haven't discovered it yet. Once you start utilizing your gift, all that changes. That's what living within your area of gifting is all about. When you tap into the power of God's Holy Spirit for His purposes, then you can exceed your natural talents and abilities and perform at superhuman levels.

Gift Wrap

- Spend more time with the Father. His instructions for increasing your gifting are written in Scripture. (Matthew 6:33)

- Take the Milestone Marketplace Gift Assessment. We offer this as part of our corporation. If you require greater guidance and accountability, sign up for Milestone Consulting.

- Listen to what others say. Often they will see the gifts in you before you will.

- Surround yourself with mentors in your area of gifting.

- When you ask for work in your area of gifting and work in a way that honors the Lord, you will perform at a superhuman level.

Darrayl's Other Gift: Faith

CHAPTER 2

THE MAGIC OF TEAMWORK

Pat Williams: Playing in the Arena of Life

Yet what we suffer now is nothing compared to the glory
he will give us later.

—ROMANS 8:18, NLT

Name: Pat Williams
Position: Senior Vice President
Company: Orlando Magic
Gift: Administration

Pat Williams was raised in Wilmington, Delaware, earned his
bachelor's degree at Wake Forest University, and his master's
at Indiana University. He was the catcher for the Wake Forest
baseball team, helping them to win the conference championship
in 1962. Then, Pat spent seven years in the United States Army
and seven with the Philadelphia Phillies organization, two as a
minor league catcher and five in the front office.

> The most important thing I did every day was walk into the clubhouse the right way. Didn't matter if we'd won eight in a row or lost eight in a row. My players needed to see an upbeat, positive, optimistic manager. If they had seen my chin down at my belt buckle that would have spread across the clubhouse like wild fire.
>
> —TOMMY LASORDA

Pat is best known for his success as an NBA general manager where he helped guide the Chicago Bulls and Atlanta Hawks to success and, ultimately, the Philadelphia 76ers to an NBA championship. As co-founder of Orlando Magic, Pat continues to serve as Senior Vice President. But his real passion is serving God and helping others become winners through Godly living.

"I'm convinced character is taught, leaders are made, and development of both begins at home. My wife and I have a large family," Pat explains. "Years ago we adopted two little girls from South Korea. The idea seemed innocent enough, but I tend to get carried away, so as the years went on, we found that we had a hard time saying 'no' to kids who needed a home. We would hear about a child here or problems in a situation over there, and our reaction was, 'Oh, why not? We can take two more.' We kept saying 'yes' and opening our home until we eventually had children falling out of every window."

Eventually, Pat and his wife, Ruth, moved into a house with 13 bedrooms and 8 bathrooms. "One year, there were 16 children—all teenagers—living under one roof," he says. "That's the year I realized why some animals eat their young. We got through it, but it wasn't easy. And neither is developing the character qualities that make you a good person and successful leader. We don't come into the world with a sense of honesty and integrity. We have to teach virtues to our kids, and we have to be aggressive about it. Our natural bent as humans is to sin, so we have to be taught character qualities, and that learning process begins at home.

> My father used to play with my brother and me in the yard. Mother would come out and say, "You're tearing up the grass." Dad would reply, "We're not raising grass. We're raising boys."
>
> —HARMON KILLEBREW

"In my mind, Dad is the key player. As I travel throughout the country speaking to groups, I hear over and over that a kid's father was the one who taught vital character qualities. Moms play a huge role in the home, but it's the father, that male influence, that teaches both in actions and words those virtues. Youth sports help. Scouting teaches character. Church obviously is a big influencer, but you can't just drop your kids off and expect them to get it. A recent study showed that 94 percent of all kids brought up in the church, left.

"So you have to constantly be there, teaching in the home. You just can't leave the business of character training to someone else. I think at the end of the day you can only go as high on the leadership ladder as your character will allow you."

And you can't wait for your leadership skills to develop. Great leaders actively develop their skills, and from Pat's years of working with sports teams and speaking to organizations, he's convinced all great leaders possess an ability to communicate passion, vision, hope, motivation and teamwork.

Communicate Your Passion

"Passion comes from loving what you do," Pat explains. "I've found in my studies that if you don't love what you do, you can fake it for two weeks. After two weeks, the jig is up. I can tell you that after 40 years in the NBA, I'm still as excited about getting up today as I was when I started. So, my advice to anyone seeking to excel is to find something that ignites you because when you're passionate about something, it spills over into the lives of those around you. Great leaders simply love what they do."

Communicate Your Vision

Great leaders also communicate their vision. Without vision, nothing happens. As a leader, your vision should be clear, simple, and easily grasped by everyone on the team. Clarity of purpose and the promise of payoff will carry your team or organization through the tough times, and when your team members buy into the vision, they become an irresistible force.

"Great leaders understand there is a price to pay now in order to reap the benefits of their future vision," Pat says. "Duke's basketball coach, Mike Krzyzewski, once told me he begins each season by explaining to his players that if they'll put aside their personal ambitions for the good of the team, the payoff will be enormous. Both for the individual player and the team."

This vision, this singular drive toward a goal, embodies the spirit of a great leader, and when the vision and persona of the leader become so intertwined that the leader becomes the vision, then others will follow, no matter what the cost.

In his book *Coaching Your Kids to Be Leaders: The Keys to Unlocking Their Potential,* Pat writes, "When Moses returned from the mountain, he found the people 'out of control.' The Bible used the same word for 'out of control' that Proverbs used for 'perish' in the statement, 'Where there is no vision, the people perish.' In other words, where there is no visionary leadership, the people are out of control. Great leaders communicate vision to their team."

Communicate Hope & Optimism

Great leaders communicate hope. They project optimism. They uplift, encourage, and forgive. President Ronald Regan said, "Optimism is a choice and one of the most powerful ones you can make."

Pat agrees. "Effective leaders use humor to convey hope and optimism and to break tension," he says. "Hope through humor keeps a team loose and confident. Napoleon said, 'A leader is a dealer in hope,' and I believe that to be true. Every day as a leader you get to make a decision. You can be an optimistic leader or a pessimistic leader. Optimism trumps pessimism every time, so project a positive attitude and your team will win."

Communicate Motivation & Inspiration

Great leaders communicate motivation. "After forty years in the NBA, I'm still longing for a team where everyone is self-motivated. Hasn't happened yet, but I'm hopeful. I remember talking to numerous opponents who'd played against Michael Jordan, and they all said the same thing: He would not quit. No matter what the score was, no matter how little time was left, they were always scared to death because with Michael, he was going to keep coming at you.

"I love that kind of drive. You're just going to tunnel under issues; you're going to pole vault over problems. Richard DeVos, the owner of the Orlando Magic and co-founder of Amway, made an interesting statement. He said, 'Perseverance is stubbornness with a purpose.' In other words, have a reason for hanging in there. You don't just hang in there foolishly; you stick with it because you see the finished product, you see the goal, and you just want it so badly you're not going to quit. That's self-motivation, and great leaders light a fire under people. They touch souls, inspire, and motivate."

Communicate Teamwork

Great leaders communicate teamwork. Grant Hill was in the weight room of the Orlando Magic one day when Pat asked him, "Grant, what's the one thing you remember about playing for Mike K at Duke?"

Grant thought for a moment and said, "Probably the fist. Coach K taught us about the fist. He would hold up his hand and say, 'These five fingers represent the five players on the court. As punching devices, as weapons, they aren't much. And in a fist, if one finger comes loose, you lose something. If two come out, you lose a lot. But as long as that fist is together, you have something that is really powerful and can cause a lot of damage.' Coach K said those five fingers represent what all teams embody: trust, communication, pride, collective responsibility, and caring. When we leave a huddle after a time out, we don't yell 'defense' or 'win.' We yell 'together.' Makes sense doesn't it, the magic of team work?"

The same leadership concepts apply to the body of Christ. "We all have special gifts," Pat says. "I think we all have a calling. I think God has His hand on His people, and He expects us to get busy for Him. He expects us to use those gifts or talents or interests. People ask me all the time, 'How do I find the will of God? What am I meant to do with my life?' Part of my answer is direct: What are you good at?

"One thing they say is, 'Oh, I love this,' but if you have no ability or background or training it's tough to use that gift. So, find out what you love to do. Then sit down in consultation with the Lord and think through what you know you love to do. If you're excited about it, that's a sign God has planted that gift in you. It's tough to do something if you're unenthusiastic. If you don't have energy or passion or drive or zeal or zest or some zing in your life, you can't just hump that up and manufacture it on your own. God gives you the drive and that thrust to do things. So, I think that's a good part of finding God's will. Organization, leadership, and encouragement are my passions, and God has blessed me with those gifts. He's allowed me to use those them in the arena of life, and I thank Him for that."

> When Jesus heard what had happened, he withdrew
> by boat privately to a solitary place. Hearing of this, the
> crowds followed him on foot from the towns.
>
> —MATTHEW 14:13, NIV

Gift Wrap

- You just can't leave the business of character training to someone else. I think at the end of

the day you can only go as high on the leadership
ladder as your character will allow you.

- Passion comes from loving what you do. I've
  found in my studies that if you don't love what
  you do, you can fake it for two weeks. After two
  weeks the jig is up.

- Optimism trumps pessimism every time, so
  project a positive attitude and your team will
  win.

Pat's Other Gifts: Leadership, Encouragement & Writing

The disciples came to him and said, 'This is a remote place,
and it's already getting late. Send the crowds away, so they
can go to the villages and buy themselves some food.'
—MATTHEW 14:15, NIV

CHAPTER 3

FOOD FOR THOUGHT

Judson Allen: A Feast Fit for a King

Jesus answered, 'It is written: People do not live on bread alone but on every word that comes from the mouth of God.

—MATTHEW 4:4, NIV

> Name: Judson Allen
> Position: Owner
> Company: Healthy Infused Cuisine
> Gift: Craftsmanship

What makes us rich? Is it our hard work and intellect that allows us to prosper? How do we create wealth? Does success come from raw effort, good luck, and connections in high places, or is there another force at work? Here's some food for thought from Judson Allen's work in the kitchen.

> Then Jesus directed them to have all the people sit down in groups on the green grass. So they sat down in groups of hundreds and fifties.
> —MARK 6:39, NIV

17

Success in Small Things

First, start with small steps. "For who hath despised the day of small thing." (Zechariah 4:10, KJV)

As a young man, Judson Allen dreamed of food. He baked bread in his head, created dishes in his sleep, and mixed, measured, and stirred ingredients until he was a master chef—at least in his imagination. For Judson, food meant fellowship, sharing a meal, a festive event. More importantly, cooking for others was an act of hospitality, linking the creator with his creation.

"One of the first things I made by myself was a chocolate pound cake," Judson says. "It was for a bake-off at our church picnic. The competition was my grandmother who, of course, made her famous brownies. I wish I could say I beat grandma, but I didn't. She took first. I won second."

For Judson, this early affirmation served as a predictor for future success. God often uses our small victories to spur us toward a larger field of work. When Jesus sought a quiet place to pray and reflect, He found the legacy of his work preceded him. The people had seen how he'd changed water into wine, healed an official's son, a leper, a centurion's servant, a paralytic, two blind men, and raised Jairus' daughter from the dead. They'd watched Him heal others, so they sought him out for his gift.

Delegate

Looking up to heaven, he gave thanks.

—MARK 6:41, NIV

Second, build your team and delegate responsibility. As you begin to work in your area of gifting, you may find that your field of influence expands. Others may seek you out, demanding your time, expertise, and personal attention. If so, pay attention to their needs. This clamor for assistance often points toward your field of ministry. Listen to the needs of others, and touch their wounds. Pray that God will allow you to work on their behalf in a supernatural way.

"You know it's one thing to cook behind the scenes and push out great meals to people in a restaurant," Judson says. "But it's another to cook in front of people and connect with them in a public way. But that's something that I love. That's what really lights my fire.

"When I speak to others, I feel God's words flowing from within me. It blows my mind because it's like God is giving me the ability to speak and connect to people. He gives me confidence, and we all need that from time to time. I've been in those situations where I haven't known what to say or how to say it, but God has truly shown me His favor and brought to mind those things I needed to recall. People may come to me afterwards and say, 'Wow, what you said truly affected me.' That's when I know it's not me but God at work."

> "How many loaves do you have?" he asked. "Go and see."
> —MARK 6:38, NIV

As God expands your realm of influence, the risk and rewards of failure and success will increase. It's during these moments when God may be calling you to enlarge your tent and assemble a staff to support your work. When Moses became overwhelmed with the complaints of the people, his father-in-law advised him to appoint judges who could act on his behalf.

Delegation frees up your time and resources, enabling you to focus on the larger mission of your work. Delegation doesn't relieve you of the responsibility of your work. It does, however, allow you to designate emissaries to act on your behalf and, thus, free you up for a greater work.

> They all ate and were satisfied.
> —MARK 6:42, NIV

Divide & Serve Smaller Portions

Third, divide the work. Separate the tasks and serve in a personal way. Taking on too much can leave you bloated by ego and burned out. Learn to say 'no' to the urgent and 'yes' to the important issues.

"You know, you hear a lot of people who go to college say, 'As a freshman I gained 10 or 15 pounds. Well for me, I gained 50. Every year I put on weight so that by the time I graduated, I weighed about 325 pounds. And for a guy who was a food scientist and a nutritionist major, that just wasn't good. It came to the point where I wasn't happy with myself at that weight. I knew that with what I was trying to do in my career and what I wanted to do in terms of my health, in order to reach those goals, I had to let the weight go.

"So, when I graduated from college I made a conscious effort to begin cooking for myself, making healthier meals and eating smaller portions. But because I enjoy the experience of eating, I wanted to prepare meals that were tasty, not some bland dish that was going to leave me craving a Whopper at Burger King. I started preparing meals that were healthy, nutritious, and enjoyable. Over a two-year period I was able to lose about 90 pounds. But, I tell people my struggle isn't over. The hardest thing wasn't necessarily losing the weight—it was keeping it off. It's saying 'no' on a daily basis."

Are you the only one who can do the urgent task? If not, find someone with the skill and knowledge that is grateful for the opportunity of a new challenge. Avoid the temptation to interfere, hover, and disrupt. Divide the work, trust your team, and find the right person for the right task at the right time.

Plan, Prepare, Pray

Fourth, plan, prepare, and pray for your success. Success begins with our hands folded and knees bent. Before we begin a new work, we should count the cost, consider the commitment, and pray for discernment. Is this opportunity really from God or just a diversion?

"I found as I grew older that serving a well prepared meal takes more than a few minutes in the kitchen. It takes hours of shopping, washing, slicing, and measuring. But for me, it's worth it because food affects the mind, body, and spirit. Cooking puts my mind at ease; it allows me to express my creativity through flavors. There's a tactile experience that resonates with our inner being when we smell the spices, taste the sauces, and allow the texture of a morsel to linger on our lips. I know for some, eating is just a way of filling the body with energy, but for me, food is an act of worship."

Work With What You Have

Fifth, begin where you are with what you have. "When I decided to begin cooking for others, I asked a friend if I could cook for him. I didn't know what I was doing. I just knew I wanted to cook, and I needed someone to serve as a guinea pig. So I said, 'Hey, let me make meals for you. I'll cook, package, and deliver them to your home. At the end of a week, let's see how your weight does. We'll see if you begin to feel an increase in energy and a decrease in blood pressure and cholesterol. So I started with what I had and went to work.

"After one week, I knew I had something big. You know there are other companies that offer a similar service, but Healthy Infused Cuisine provides upscale gourmet meals delivered to your home. We also provide personal chef services which is different than a catering service. By just taking what the Lord gave me and using the gifts of His spirit, I was able to turn my passion for cooking into a business."

A Feast Fit for a King

Whatever God calls you to do, whatever talents you receive, "... work at it with all your heart, as working for the Lord." (Colossians 3:23, New International Version)

"With cooking, I'm using my hands and the creative side of my brain. It allows me to construct beautifully created dishes. One of the myths I try to dispel is that healthy food is boring. Using ingredients like fresh herbs, olive oil, garlic, rice wine vinegar, and red pepper flakes can awaken a dish and provide a great eating experience. And I believe that's the life to which Christ calls us, one that's exciting, beautiful, and spicy. When you're working within your spiritual gifting, you too awaken and come alive. For me, that's the essence of abundant living." The metaphor of food permeates the Bible. Jesus is the bread of life, manna sustained a nation in the desert for forty years, and God told his people to prepare a meal on the night they left Egypt. Christ began his ministry with a miracle at a wedding feast and concluded his work with an intimate meal shared with his disciples in an upper room.

"I know that some see what I do as cooking," Judson says, "but it's much more than that. It's fellowship. It's worship. It's bonding with God in the most primal way. For me, cooking is an act of craftsmanship. Whenever I cook at an event or present a dish, I bring it before God. That really sums up how I approach my work."

> A champion is someone who gets up when he can't.
> —JACK DEMPSEY

Gift Wrap

- By just taking what the Lord gave me and using the gifts of His spirit, I was able to turn my passion for cooking into a business."

- When you're working within your spiritual gifting, you too awaken and come alive."

- Christ began his ministry with a miracle at a wedding feast and concluded his work with an intimate meal shared with his disciples in an upper room.

Judson's Other Gift: Teaching

CHAPTER 4

WHEN BUSINESS AS USUAL WON'T CUT IT!

Dave Kahle: Position Yourselves With Power

Do not merely listen to the word, and so deceive yourselves. Do what it says.

—JAMES 1:22, NLT

Name: Dave Kahle
Position: Founder
Company: The DaCo Corporation
Gift: Writing

The plastic chair rocked slightly as Molly shifted the briefcase in her lap and eyed her sales report. Gross sales up slightly, profits down. Down too, her ranking within the sales force. The looming consolidation of sales territories meant she'd need a bump, and a big one, if she were to survive the next round of cuts. She snapped shut her briefcase and silently practiced her sales pitch. An air conditioning vent chilled the backs of her legs. The plastic potted plant provided a buffer between her and the other sales executives waiting with her in the lobby. Two she recognized as direct competitors, and among them was the facility's preferred vendor.

The sliding glass door at the receptionist desk slid open. Molly heard her name called. She stood, smoothed the wrinkles from her dark blue skirt, and marched down the hall toward the purchasing department. But she already knew she had no chance of landing the account—no chance at all.

"One of the basic truths in sales is that good salespeople sell more than average salespeople" says Dave Kahle. "I've been selling for—well, for a long time. And almost every day, if not every week, I say to myself, 'Dave, you could've done that better.' I'm firmly convinced it's not just good career advice, it's a spiritual and ethical obligation.

"We are each given certain gifts and talents, and we have an ethical obligation to unleash them to the fullest extent that we can. Every salesperson is hired for their future contribution, not for their past performance. They're hired for what they can bring in business, goodwill, and profit. So if you don't accept your responsibility to improve and excel, you are in effect robbing your employer.

"A number of years ago the National Society of Sales Training Executives did a study on the characteristics within every industry and identified the top five percent of sales superstars. The number one behavioral characteristic among top producers is that they see the situation from the customer's point of view, not their own. They also ask better questions, listen more constructively, land bigger deals, and are obsessed with time management. Asking questions and listening, what can be more basic than that? And yet top performers do it better than the rest.

"That's why in my book *Take Your Sales Performance Up A Notch,* I examine the different areas of a salesperson's job and break them down into core competencies. For example, asking questions is a competency. Listening is a competency. Time management is a competency. So we group the competencies into categories and explain how to become an effective salesperson using these skills. Underlying our approach is the expectation that we can all become better in every area of sales. Now that might sound simple, but honestly a great percentage of the sales people have never really grasped that they can and should continually improve. To me, skill development is more than just a business issue, it's an ethical responsibility."

The Buying Process

One of the first steps you can take to improve your sales success is to master the buying process.

"Consider the decisions a customer must make in the buying process. First they must decide whether or not to phone your company as a result of an advertisement. If they decide not to, you never hear from them. But if they contact you, then they've moved to step two.

"Second, they must decide whether to interact honestly with you. Let's say they reach you on the phone. In the first few moments of a call, the customer will make a subconscious decision as to how candid they will be with you. You know that because you've been in the same position as a buyer and dealt with sales people who are curt, abrasive, or unconcerned about you. Chances are you didn't spend a lot of time describing your situation. It's the same with your customers. They must make a decision to interact honestly with you before the sales process can go forward. Once they've decided to interact with you, you're probably going to ask for an appointment to see them.

"Third, they will decide to meet with you. If they agree to a meeting then their fourth decision is whether or not to keep the appointment they made with you. If they don't keep the appointment, you've wasted your time and your job becomes more complicated. So before you can influence them to spend money with you, you must influence them to keep the appointment they made.

"Let's say they keep the appointment. Finally, they must decide whether or not to converse truthfully and thoroughly with you. If they don't trust you, don't like you, or find something about you that makes them uncomfortable or suspicious, they won't want to engage. Without a positive decision at this point in the relationship, you'll never have the opportunity to present them with the final decision, which is to say yes or no to your offer. In a very simplified manner this is how all customers operate."

Selling Yourself

Given the current economic conditions, high unemployment rate, and increased global competition, a large segment of the population struggles to find steady work. Many people have turned to freelancing or starting their own companies. But Dave says that even freelancers and entrepreneurs need basic sales skills to compete and be successful.

"As a freelancer you try to find a lot of small jobs that require your gifts and talents. A small business owner may start out with a small pool of clients. But whether you're trying to land a multi-million dollar contract or a small home repair job, the heart of the sales process remains the conversation you have with your customers and prospective clients. It's that moment where you are face to face with the customer that defines the uniqueness of your position and distinguishes you from all the others who are competing for that sale. If you're going to be a skillful influencer, you must master this process.

"When you speak with your customers your goal is to:

- Make them comfortable with you.
- Discover what they want.
- Describe what you offer.
- Show how what you have helps them get what they want.
- Get their agreement to take the next step.

"That simple five-step process is the basis of every interaction you have with your customer. It's the heart of influencing. It can take months to complete in an intricate sales process, or it can be whisked through in two minutes over the phone. For example, in the initial phone call or meeting, the potential client has only two decisions to make: interact honestly and thoroughly with you, and make an appointment with you.

"Your job as the salesperson is to facilitate those two decisions. You do this by making them feel comfortable with you. This helps with their first decision. Then you listen to their story and present to them their need to make an appointment with you. Finally, you ask for the appointment. That leads to their next decision. In this short (two-to-five minute phone call,) you've progressed through each of the five basic steps."

Managing the Sales Interaction

Your primary role as sales executive or businessperson is not to present information. Rather, your primary role is to manage the communication process between you and your customer. Without a two-way conversation between you and the customer, the sales process isn't viable.

Dave explains, "Managing the sales interaction means the two of you are moving toward an agreement. My definition of sales is this: influencing a customer to come to an agreement with you to purchase something you offer. The agreement is the main thing. A conversation that moves toward agreement is a dialogue. That means it's an honest exchange of feelings, facts, values, and perceptions. The depth and quality of that interaction and communication is the distinguishing standard."

Called to Communicate

Despite his success as a salesman, Dave views himself as a communicator who uses spoken and printed words to convey his message and effect change in the minds of his readers and clients.

"Early on I felt I had a gift of writing. I list it as a subcategory under wisdom and teaching. As an adolescent, when someone would ask me what I wanted to be when I grew up, I would say without hesitation that I wanted to be a writer. Today, I write a lot.

I have my ninth book coming out in December. I write one article a week for an e-zine, and I also write specific assignments for various publications. It's my writing that has allowed me to carve out a place in this world. My weekly article reaches over 40,000 people, so there is a significant responsibility on my part to deliver a message that has value.

"That's why I consider writing a gift and not a skill. Here's what I mean by gift. Often I'll get an idea for an article or maybe just a word or phrase. But it's never more developed than that. Rarely do I get a fully formed paragraph. From there I'll just put it in my sub-conscious and allow it to lodge itself into the back of my mind. At some point, maybe within the next couple of weeks, I'll sit down to write. Usually within an hour I will have written a 1,000 to 1,500 words on that topic. The next day I come back and edit a little, but pretty soon it takes shape as a publishable piece. That's how I know it's not me; it's God in me. So for me, writing is a gift.

"In addition to this gift of writing I also speak, teach, and train others in the art of communicating. For example, I'll be in Texas one week, Wisconsin the next, and Baton Rouge after that. It's just what I do; I educate groups of people in the art of influencing through words. But there's nothing in my background that would lead you, me, or anyone else to believe that I could do that effectively. So I know this craft of words and communication is truly a gift."

Gaining the Advantage

Fast, Good, and Cheap, Pick Two, the sign reads outside a print shop. But do the old rules still apply? Dave argues that in today's competitive culture, you need to go beyond the accepted limitations of the past and develop your own advantage, an advantage buried in an opportunity disguised as a problem.

"At one time I sold surgical staplers," Dave says. "Part of the process was to train surgeons in how to use these instruments in surgery. But in order to do this the salesperson had to work one-on-one with the surgeon. This made for a very intense environment. One of the things that I did to reduce the tension and expedite the training process was to present small seminars. I would teach five or six surgeons at a time. This allowed them to relax and grasp the mechanics of the tool in a stress-free environment. These seminars also gave me the chance to redefine my job. I went from being an instructor of one to a teacher of many, and thus immediately expanded my territory.

"This concept of problem solving is precisely how I became a writer. As a salesman, any time somebody needed a letter or a sell sheet written, I would volunteer. I would offer to help not because I thought it might lead somewhere but because I just wanted an opportunity to exercise what I was beginning to see as something I enjoyed. At that point, I hadn't really identified writing as a gift yet. It was more an urge.

"This is why I advise others who want to exercise their gifts in the marketplace to look for problems. The other key to developing your gift is to look for situations or types of people for which you have empathy. It is the combination of your gift and your purpose that defines your market. Ask yourself, 'Who do I have empathy for? Who do I have some connection with? What groups can I help?'

"I believe you have an obligation to your Creator to do the absolute best job that you can regardless of circumstances you find yourself in. It's a fundamental piece of spiritual insight. We're each given certain gifts and talents, and we have an ethical obligation to unleash them to the fullest extent that we can. As an example, for most of my career as a writer and a sales educator, I have had ideas that I believe came from God. To do anything less than my best is an affront to the one who empowers me. So my advice is this: Unleash your gifts and aim them toward every problem you confront. Do that, and you'll find yourself in a position of power."

Gift Wrap

- The heart of the sales process remains the conversation you have with your customers and prospective clients. It's that moment where you are face to face with the customer that defines the uniqueness of your position and distinguishes you from all the others who are competing for that sale. If you're going to be a skillful influencer, you must master this process.

- Your primary role as sales executive or businessperson is not to present information. Rather, your primary role is to manage the communication process between you and your customer.

- In today's competitive culture, you need to go beyond the accepted limitations of the past and develop your own advantage, an advantage buried in an opportunity disguised as a problem.

Dave's Other Gift: Teaching

CHAPTER 5

LISTEN TO THE MAN IN YOUR CORNER

George Foreman: Knock Them Out With Love

Blessed are the meek, for they will inherit the earth.

—MATTHEW 5:5, NIV

> Name: George Foreman
> Position: Former Heavyweight Boxing Champion
> Company: George Foreman Enterprises, Inc.
> Gift: Discernment

January 22, 1973: With his wife and daughters in Austin, Texas, former President Lyndon Baines Johnson sits alone in his bedroom at his ranch in Johnson City, Texas, bristling at the news that President Nixon (and not Johnson) has arranged for a cease-fire with North Vietnam. Suddenly Johnson's left arm goes numb. Seconds later a wave of nausea sweeps over him. He rolls across the bed and reaches for the phone, fearing the pain in his chest is the beginning of a third heart attack.

Meanwhile, in Washington, D.C., another Texan, Dallas County District Attorney Henry Wade, listens in stunned silence as the U.S. Supreme Court rules against Wade and the state of Texas. In a 7-2 decision, the court overturns Texas' law forbidding abortions and rules that "Jane Roe" (Norma McCorvey) has the right to terminate the life of her unborn child.

In the days and weeks to come, the news of these two events will dominate the headlines, but on this night another Texan claims the spotlight. In Kingston, Jamaica, a young boxer named George Foreman is about to battle for the heavyweight boxing title.

Joe Frazier is the champion and a 3–1 favorite to defeat his younger challenger, even though Foreman carries a higher ranking (second). But it is the top-ranked contender Muhammad Ali that most viewers want to see. For months the public has clamored for a Frazier-Ali rematch. Frazier, however, has refused to split the $6-million payout. "Smoking Joe" feels his status as reigning champion commands a larger share of the prize money. Ali's camp contends it's Ali and not Frazier who the viewers flock to see.

With both sides deadlocked, Frazier has agreed to fight Foreman on a warm night in the tropics. In return, Frazier will receive a guaranteed $800,000 purse, instead of the $3 million he would have collected by fighting Ali. The bell rings and round one begins with Frazier pressing Foreman as the champ tries to land body shots. Frazier lands a hard shot to the head, but Foreman seems unfazed. A minute into the round, Foreman begins to find his rhythm. He starts pushing Frazier away, keeping the champ at arm's length. Each time Frazier approaches, Foreman pushes back, providing the challenger with the space he needs to land his jab. At the two-minute mark, with the crowd yelling, "Ice 'em Joe. Ice 'em!" Foreman stuns Frazier with a swift uppercut that catches the champ in mid-step. Frazier stumbles, falling onto the seat of his pants. Frazier quickly bounces up, but it's Foreman who remains the aggressor. He knocks Frazier back on the ropes and pounds him with a combination of body blows. Another vicious right uppercut catches Frazier flush on the chin, and he goes down again. Ringside announcer Howard Cosell can't believe how easily Foreman is handling Frazier. To the viewers watching on closed-circuit TV, "Smoking Joe" appears sluggish and slow. Frazier stands again, but just before the bell, Foreman unleashes another barrage of hits and drops the champ for the third time in the first round. At the standing count of five, the bell rings, and the two men return to their corners, one wounded and wobbly, the other energized and on the cusp of stunning success.

"If you're going to be a champion, you're going to get knocked down," George says. "That's just the way it is. And chances are, you're going to get knocked down a lot; everyone does. But the great ones get back up. They wipe away the tears and blood and fight on."

As an amateur, Foreman had knocked out L.C. Brown to win the San Francisco Examiner's Senior Title in San Francisco in 1968. In March of that year, he won four fights, three by knockout, to win the National AAU Heavyweight title. Later that same year, he went 2–1 against the West German team in Germany and won a decision over Otis Evans to make the U.S. boxing team. During the summer

Olympics in Mexico City, Foreman knocked out Russia's Ionas Chepulis to win the Olympic Games Heavyweight Gold Medal.

"After winning gold at the Olympics, I turned pro," George says. "I remember thinking, *This is going to be the easiest thing I've ever done.* As soon as I stepped into the ring I got knocked down hard. I remember laying there, looking past the ropes at these women, five or six of them, all wearing fur coats—the exact same type of fur coat. And I remember thinking, *That's odd: All them ladies dressed the same.* Then I hear the referee counting. 'Four, five, six.' But I'm still on my back, watching those women in the fur coats. Only now there's three of them. And then two. And finally there's just the one.

"That was my introduction to boxing. It was also my introduction to what it takes to make it as a businessman. I learned early on that if you're going to succeed, you have to know how to take a punch. That's just the way it is in boxing and life. In the seventies, I became a pretty successful professional boxer. I won the title and made a lot of money. Then in the eighties, I thought to myself, *Boxing can't be my thing forever.* I needed to find another way to support my family after the glamour of boxing faded. So I went into a lot of businesses. Most of them failed. That's when I learned that boxing and business are a lot alike. If you want to be a winner, you need to have great people in your corner."

> Being humble does not mean you think less of yourself
> or that you're beneath people. People with humility don't
> think less of themselves. They just think of themselves less.
> —Anonymous

The Trainer

"First, you need a trainer in your corner, someone with vision. Early on in my business dealings, I didn't have that person looking out for me, and I got beat up pretty good.

"As a boxer you really aren't the best judge of how well you're handling the fight. A boxer is focused on one thing: hitting the guy in front of him. But his trainer sees the big picture. He knows who's winning on points, how the ref is handling the match, and if his man is tiring. The trainer will say, 'Slow down. Conserve your energy.' Or he'll encourage you to pour it on and lay it all out there because he can see that the other fellow is in trouble. In life and business you need a trainer, someone who's preparing you for the tough times ahead. You need someone who can see things objectively and is willing to tell you the hard truth.

"One reason why I had to get back into boxing is I didn't have someone in my business corner, and I'd lost a lot of money. But I knew I could be a successful boxer again, so in the eighties I stepped back into the ring. Even though I was winning matches and moving up in the rankings, I was still looking for that next big thing that would provide for my family. And to be honest with you, when that opportunity came along, I almost missed it.

"Someone had come to me pitching the idea of this cooking grill. But I couldn't see how this thing was going to make me any money. But my wife overheard the conversation and said, 'George, the grill works. I've tried it. And it's great. All you have to do is put your meat right there.' Then she put a hamburger on the grill, and I watched the grease melt away. Of course, I'm thinking, *Well, when the grease goes, the flavor goes, too.* But then she fixed that burger, and it was the best one I'd ever eaten.

"I came to believe in that grill the same way I believed in my boxing skills. And I knew that if I really believed in it, I could sell it. That's one of the things boxing had taught me about business: you have to be able to sell yourself to others. I knew, win or lose, if I gave 100 percent effort, people would pay to watch me fight. I was able to transfer the same enthusiasm for boxing into the promotion of the George Foreman Grill. Even after I lost a split-decision fight to Shannon Briggs in 1997, I knew I'd won when sports announcer Larry Merchant began talking about how much weight I'd dropped because of the George Foreman Grill. After that fight, sales took off. So for me, the first thing you need in business is someone with vision, a trainer who can prepare you for the big matches and opportunities."

The Scout

"The second thing you need is a scout in your corner," George says, "someone who knows the opposition and can spot your competitor's weaknesses. He's also the one who points out your weak spots. He may say, 'Keep your hands up. Move your feet. Stop standing. Bob and feign.' Your scout is your strategist. He's the one who sees the fight objectively and helps you execute your strategy.

"For example, in 1974 I was in Africa fighting Mohammed Ali. In the early rounds I beat him up pretty good, but then he starts to get my rhythm, and I can't land a shot. He keeps leaning on the ropes, covering up. Later they came to call it the "rope a dope." But that night it was me who was the dope because once he got his confidence and got to talking to me, I lost the match. He was saying things like, 'I'm gonna drop you, sucka. Look out, now. Here it comes. Look out.' "And I'm thinking, *This guy's so cocky. He's left himself wide open.* Then, just as I'm getting ready to nail him, his trainer Angelo Dundee screams at Ali to stop clowning around. Ali covers up, and I never got another chance to land a punch. He refocused.

"I never forgot that. I thought, *Man, I wish I had someone looking out for me like that.* Twenty years after that match, I had Angelo Dundee in my corner helping me to become the oldest man ever to become a heavyweight champion. That's what you have to do in business. You have to find smart people who can help you stay focused. Today, in my business, that person is my accountant. He keeps me from looking like a dope, from being sucka punched."

The Cut Man

"Finally you need a cut man, someone who will patch you up. We all get bloodied and bruised. The job of your cut man is to make sure your wounds don't get worse. In boxing, the cut man doesn't talk. He just looks for trouble spots and fixes you up. In my business, my lawyer is my cut man. When things get messy, he steps in and stops the bleeding."

Blessed Are the Meek, Not Boastful

Above all else, George believes we should be both humble in victory and gracious in defeat. "One of my favorite Bible verses is 'Blessed are the meek, for they shall inherit the earth.' It doesn't say they will conquer the earth but that they will inherit it. It's not necessary to destroy another person's business, career, relationships, or reputation just so you can succeed. You don't have to coerce, steal, or cheat to get what you want. Meekness is not weakness. Meekness is power under control. And if you run your business God's way, you'll inherit success His way. You might not win every match, but if you do win, you'll win the right way. You can be strong and powerful and still remain under control and humble. I always tried to keep that in mind when I was boxing. I never wanted to hurt my opponent. I just wanted to win, and most times I did."

January 22, 1973, Kingston, Jamaica: The bell rings announcing the start of the second round. Foreman moves to the center of the ring, but it's not long before he drops Frazier a forth time. Those near the ring can hear Foreman yelling to Frazier's manager, Yancy Durham, to stop the fight. Frazier's hurt, his eyes are unfocused. But Durham and Frazier refuse to quit. The champ crawls to his feet and plods toward Foreman, still trying to crowd the contender, still trying to bring the heat. But the smoke has gone out of Joe. Another blow to the body and Frazier goes down, wobbles to his feet, and waits for the mandatory eight count. Foreman is all business. His goal now is to end the fight. If Frazier's corner won't save their boxer, Foreman will. Foreman tags Frazier in the head and follows with a right cross that pitches the champ onto one knee. He sits up at the count of three, his eyes, glassy; his face, swollen. On his feet, he stumbles to a corner but the ref had seen enough. He calls the fight. The world has a new heavyweight champion. And Texans have reason again to feel proud of one of their own.

Australians are balanced people. We have a chip on each shoulder.

—PETER J. DANIELS

Gift Wrap

- If you're going to be a champion, you're going to get knocked down. That's just the way it is. And chances are, you're going to get knocked down a lot; everyone does. But the great ones get back up. They wipe away the tears and blood and fight on.

- Boxing and business are a lot alike. If you want to be a winner, you need to have great people in your corner.

- In life and business you need a trainer, someone who's preparing you for the tough times ahead. You need someone who can see things objectively and is willing to tell you the hard truth.

- One of the things boxing had taught me about business: you have to be able to sell yourself to others. I knew, win or lose, if I gave 100 percent effort, people would pay to watch me fight. I was able to transfer the same enthusiasm for boxing into the promotion of the George Foreman Grill.

George's Other Gift: Faith

> My family had never made a mark. Most had enjoyed free
> board and lodging with King George the sixth. In short,
> they were in jail.
>
> —PETER J. DANIELS

CHAPTER 6

I'M YOUR WAKE UP CALL

Peter J. Daniels: Turn Back On Your Dream Machine

Do not let this Book of the Law depart from your mouth;
meditate on it day and night, so that you may be careful to
do everything written in it. Then you will be prosperous
and successful.

—JOSHUA 1:5, NIV

> Name: Peter J. Daniels
> Position: Founder
> Company: Dan El Private Estates
> Gift: Leadership

What do you do when your dreams fail? You get a
new dream.

—PETER J. DANIELS

The young teen recognized the taste of hunger. The grumbling
in his belly left an odd flavor in his mouth, like a leafy green
vegetable that had turned rancid. It was this familiar ache and tang

in his gut that led him to the old woman's home. From the street, he'd smelled the rolls baking in the oven. Now he stood in the shadows of a darkened back porch peering through a screen door. His mouth salivated at the sight of shimmering patties of butter melting into the golden-brown crusts. Too afraid to knock and too proud to steal, he merely stood on the stoop inhaling the aroma. The heavy plodding of the woman's footsteps returning to the kitchen drove him off the porch and back into the yard. A motorcar rumbled past, kicking up a wake of fine red dust that coated his skin. He watched the red tail lights for a long time, wishing his family had a motorcar. Or a home. Or food.

He returned to the roadway and eyed the street signs, desperately trying to read the words. But the letters merely appeared as random symbols, their meanings lost on him. Lost. That summed up his existence. Even if he were to find his way back to the shack, he'd still be lost. Neither he nor the others who occupied the temporary dwelling could help him find his way out of the poverty that pulled him deeper into darkness.

The light went out in the kitchen. He heard the squeak of a door slowly shutting. The snap of a metal lock dropping into place prompted him to turn back toward the motorway. Shoving his hands into his threadbare pants, he lowered his head and trudged barefoot into the night. Only the stars in the southern sky shown the way, and soon those, too, winked off as an approaching rainstorm moved across eastern Australia. Moments later, his tears became mixed with the rain, and the young teen wondered, *Does God weep when he sees a starving boy*? He hoped so. God, he hoped so.

I've never had the disadvantage of going to university.
—Peter J. Daniels

Though Peter J. Daniels was never so bad off that he felt tempted to steal, he knows what it's like to be poor. He was, in his own words, "So far in debt [he] had to reach up to touch bottom." Alcoholism had run in Peter's family, so he had little hope of escaping the whirlpool that had gripped his family for three generations. As a child, Peter suffered from acute dyslexia. School officials considered his condition so severe that they recommended he be housed in a class with children who had suffered from brain damage. A debilitating bout of diphtheria left him weak, putting him further behind in his studies. He failed every grade in school and sought work as a bricklayer and mason. But though he trailed his peers intellectually and economically, Peter possessed a deep sense that he was meant for more, much more. And he was right. On May 25, 1959, at the age of 26, Peter attended a Billy Graham crusade. That one decision changed his life and the lives of thousands.

"That evening, I made a commitment to Christ and that decision revolutionized my life," says Peter. "I walked in illiterate and lost with little hope of escaping my circumstances. When I marched out, I was an entirely different person. I suddenly realized that in God's eyes, I was equal with all men. I reasoned that if I was the son of a king, then I needn't appear inferior to anyone. Certainly I didn't become intellectually brilliant overnight. But I did become convinced I'd be more than I was. I purchased three dictionaries, and though I couldn't read, I would point at words and get people to tell me what they meant. For five years, I listened to British broadcasting in order to get impeccable in my English. I studied law, accounting, philosophy, theology, modern and ancient history, politics and economics, and read over 2,000 biographies."

Peter went into business three times. Each time his business failed. His wife begged him to get a regular job with a steady salary, but Peter had a vision—a God-given determination to make his mark in the world, something no one in his family had ever done. In time he built a large real estate business in Australia and South East Asia. Today, Peter J. Daniels serves as a director and chairman on a range of international boards. But before the success, there were the hungry nights and daydreams.

Divine Dreams

"Soon after my transformation at the Billy Graham crusade," Peter says, "God gave me two dreams. One was to see how much money a single individual could give away in a lifetime. Now understand, at that time I received this dream, I was very poor. Nevertheless, I believed God had placed these two dreams in my heart. Today, our corporation extends into about 30 countries, and we have a no overdraft, no lines of credit, no mortgages, and our own currency."

Peter's second dream to change the world for generations to come took longer to develop. "About 20 years ago, we felt the Lord calling us to do something for the Americans. Certainly America had done so much for the rest of the world, and we felt God was asking us to help them because if America fell, then God help Christendom. And so 20 years ago, my wife and I made a commitment that we would go to fifty churches in the United States and train people in entrepreneurship. Our services would be free of charge. We'd cover our hotel bills, airfares, all expenses, and refuse any honorarium offered. We felt so strongly that Christians needed to begin winning in the marketplace again that we were willing to give generously of our time and knowledge in order to bring America back to God's economic principles. Well, the program got a little out of hand, but when we finished, we'd been to over 1,000 churches throughout the world and created more millionaires in the Christian church than anyone in history."

> You know you're born for something great. You know you're not here to be employment fodder. You're here to do something great.
>
> —PETER J. DANIELS

> Christians don't have a good name in the marketplace. They say we're lazy. They say we lack ambition. They say we talk about faith, sing about it, pray about it, preach about it, read about it, and then we go get the job with the most security in it.
>
> —PETER J. DANIELS

Seek First His Kingdom

"I'm a Bible student, not a scholar," explains Peter. "As a matter of fact, when I came to Christ, I met a Bible teacher that put his arm around me, and for the next 15 years, for two and a half hours every Saturday morning, he taught me the Bible and about faith and prayer. And I believe we need to get back to the proper ratio that God has placed before us. Even in weakness, we are strong. If the Christian church were to remove its voluntary help for the sick, the hurting, the disadvantaged, then the great captains of industry, the leaders of the trade unions, the nation's economists, and the government leaders would find that the economy would collapse and be in chaos within 90 days. The church has always been the great, silent, unsung hero of every generation. Our protection and prosperity does not come from the sword or a microchip or factories but from the hand of God. We are moving toward a new era of Christian development that has deep roots in Biblical history. When the Magi visited Jesus, they brought with them a treasure worth 400 million American dollars and laid it as his feet. The poverty mentality that has afflicted Christians in wealthy nations is a master stroke of satanic genius. It has impoverished us for decades. It has denied that every Christian is of royal blood.

"The Bible says that a man that doesn't take care of his own family is worse than an infidel and has denied the faith. You can't look after your family without having some finances to do it, and I believe God is calling us to rise up as entrepreneurs and return to His truth in order that we may be able to pass the baton of prosperity to the generations that follow. But to do that, we're going to need leaders. Will you lead?"

Leadership is Total Life

Leadership is a high calling. Leadership is not grandstanding on a platform. It is lifelong commitment. "Leadership is a willingness to accept full responsibility for the outcome," says Peter. "Leadership is climbing when others are falling. Leadership demands vision, hope, and total commitment. God works through optimists, and we are not the downtrodden; we are the uplifted. We are not pigmies; we are giants. Our cry to God ought to be that he give us gumption, action, and victory. God is committed to our development, so commit to persevere. Are you committed?"

Leadership Must Be Fearless

Leadership leaves no room for fear. "When I think of someone facing down fear," Peter says, "I think of Paul. The scriptures tell us he was beaten, imprisoned, shipwrecked, stoned, abandoned, left for dead. And yet he refused to denounce his savior Jesus Christ. You need a gun, a whip, and a chair to handle a guy like that. If you're going to be a leader, you need to be above bickering and petty gossip. You have to be occupied by the final goal and not preoccupied by the other groups. Leaders exercise creative imagination. The Bible says, "As a man thinketh in his heart, so he becomes." We begin to get the picture that from God's point of view, we become what we think about. You must not be intimidated or put down by who or what you're up against. Are you courageous?"

Leadership Demands a Different Morality

Leaders have a higher moral code. "Leaders are the first to arrive and the last to leave. Leaders are the first to give, the first to lend aid, the first to lift up, the first to encourage, and the last to be served. You can't lead from the rear. Are you up front, upstanding, and advancing a morality different than what you see around you?"

Leadership is a Lonely Business

Leadership is a lonely existence. Others see the commitment necessary and refuse to pay the price. Leadership is lonely because vision is personal. Leadership is lonely because leaders are often misunderstood. Leadership is lonely because leaders have very few counselors on their wavelength.

"When I first went into real estate years ago, I had a problem, and I called my staff together. I told them about the problem, and they all left. They wanted security. 'Well,' I said to myself, 'I'll never do that again.' Next time I had a problem, I told my bank manager. He cut off my supply of credit. I thought, *Won't do that again, either.* Next time I had a problem, I told my competitors. They were happy to hear about it. That's why to be a leader you have to develop a vertical relationship with the Savior. Is it Biblical? Oh, you bet it is. Jonah was alone in the belly of a whale; Jacob wrestled alone with the angel; John the Baptist lived alone in the desert; Moses was left alone on Mt. Sinai; Daniel was alone in the Lion's Den; Nehemiah went alone before the king; David advanced alone before Goliath; Paul was alone in prison; and Jesus prayed alone in the Garden of Gethsemane. Will you risk the solitude that comes with being a leader?"

The Gabriel Call

At times the mass media has called Peter "an adrenaline-charged salesman, a religious nut, and a battle-scarred champion against pornography." Thousands flock to hear him speak. His books sell at a frantic pace, and his recorded presentation on encouragement has sold over one million downloads. Peter's gift for creating simple business formulas to solve difficult problems means he's constantly in demand as a consultant.

"A while back," says Peter, "God revealed to me The Gabriel Call. This is an eight-week program taught in local churches. Our goal is to have over one million people tithing into their local churches and looking after their own families. Already we have three countries that want to do a trade fair. We have about 1,500 to 2,000 entrepreneurs and are building to the one million mark. Any church can participate, but they must have 20 people committed to following the program. But let me be clear. This isn't about teaching people to be teachers or life-long students. Within 12 months you have to move out into the marketplace and get on with the business of being in business."

Part of The Gabriel Call is an individual assessment of how you are using the gifts God has given you. Peter recommends each participant ask these key questions:

- At what age did you search yourself in order to discern your core potential?

- Have you asked God how you might maximize your life?

- Can you describe in 50 pages what your full potential is in every area of your life?

- If you accept that your full potential is 100 percent, at what percentage would you rate yourself right now? Twenty-five percent? Fifty? One hundred?

- If you are working at less than your full potential, what are your plans for making up the shortfall?

- When will you reach your full potential?

"God gave me this concept of The Gabriel Call almost half a century ago, back at a time when I was still poor and hungry," Peter says. "I was still just a young Christian struggling to understand my calling, but I'm convinced God did and has called me to change the world. I realize that's a crazy comment to make. I mean, how can one person change the world in their lifetime? Well, Abraham changed the world in his lifetime. Moses changed the world in his lifetime. Henry Ford changed the world in his lifetime. I believe if we can change the marketplace, we can change the world. Have you been summoned? If you have, I'm your wake up call."

> Character cannot be developed in ease and quiet. Only through experience of trial and suffering can the soul be strengthened, ambition inspired, and success achieved.
>
> —HELEN KELLER

Gift Wrap

- You can't look after your family without having some finances to do it, and I believe God is calling us to rise up as entrepreneurs and return to His truth in order that we may be able to pass the baton of prosperity to the generations that follow.

- Leadership is a high calling. Leadership is not grandstanding on a platform.

- Leaders are the first to give, the first to lend aid, the first to lift up, the first to encourage, and the last to be served.

Peter's Other Gifts: Encouragement and Teaching

CHAPTER 7

RIDICULOUS FAITH

Shundrawn Thomas: Go in the Strength You Have

For therein is the righteousness of God revealed from
faith to faith: as it is written, The just shall live by faith.

—ROMANS 1:17, KJV

> Name: Shundrawn Thomas
> Position: Speaker, Author & Executive
> Company: Ridiculous Faith
> Gift: Faith

You keep him in perfect peace whose mind is stayed on
you, because he trusts in you.

—ISAIAH 26:3, ESV

Late 1960s: Shundrawn Thomas plopped down in front of the
television. His favorite show was about to begin. He loved the
way the businessman on the show carried a briefcase full of important documents. The dark suit looked expensive, and the shirt

cuffs, starched. The man had an air of confidence about him, of success. Each week Shundrawn watched the show and longed to be like the man on television.

When it came time for college, Shundrawn excelled. With the encouragement of his parents, he worked hard, graduating from Florida A & M with a business degree. A few years later, he received his masters from the University of Chicago Booth School of Business. After a series of career moves, he became Senior Vice President and Head of Corporate Strategy at Northern Trust Corporation.

"When you're a kid," Shundrawn says, "and people ask you what you want to be when you grow up, most times kids will say, 'I want to be a doctor or a lawyer.' Well, when someone would ask me, I'd always say I wanted to be a businessman. I didn't have people in my immediate or extended family that were very involved in business, so my first exposure to the business world was through television. I'd see these people on TV shows, and they would be wearing their suits and carrying their briefcases and going to meetings, and in my mind these people looked like they were doing something really important. What I didn't understand then, and what I do now, is that's how I'm wired. That's my makeup.

"As I got into high school, I had an opportunity to take some early business courses in accounting and applied finance, and I think that kind of solidified my interest in business. It's funny how I started out just seeing those images on TV and not necessarily knowing at that point what it all meant, but I can see now how God was shaping me, even back then. He was grooming me to become a leader and teacher.

"The older I got, the more I realized it didn't matter whether I was at work, home, or in school. I was just naturally led to teach others. Now part of this, I suppose, is that I'm intellectually curious, so I've always just been a learner. But I've always had this ability to understand complex concepts and break things down in simple ways that I can explain to others. I would say that's been helpful in a lot of different environments, including my professional career. Certainly I use that in my ministry, and I've always been very involved in teaching ministries at church."

Even though Shundrawn knew what he wanted to become when he grew up, success came slowly. "Have you ever been frustrated by circumstances, uncertain about your life's purpose, or discouraged? That was me. After college and several years in the workforce, I'd reached a level of success, but what I really wanted to do was write a book. I wanted to share my knowledge with others and give them hope. So, I took a leap of faith and left a lucrative position at a premier investment banking firm in order to pursue another of my childhood dreams. When I did, I thought God would bless me for my boldness. He didn't.

"Years passed, and all I had to show for my step of faith was a depleted bank account, a marginally successful book project, and a declining retail business. I began to question whether I'd really heard God when He'd told me to pursue my dream of writing. It was at this critical juncture in my spiritual journey that God spoke, encouraging me to study the faith of others."

From Shundrawn's examination of faith, hope, and despair, he wrote the popular book *Ridiculous Faith: Ordinary People Living Extraordinary Lives*. The book presents stories of real people with real doubts and real shortcomings—and a real God who delivers on His promises.

"God showed me how my anxiety, fear, doubt, and questioning were preventing me from enjoying a closer relationship with Him. Although I thought I understood faith, I hadn't learned to totally trust in Him. This revelation transformed my perspective about faith. I now can personally attest that God takes pleasure in doing extraordinary things through the lives of ordinary people."

For years, Shundrawn had attempted to walk with God based on some misconceptions of how faith works. He'd maintained a positive outlook and felt secure in his relationship with God, but he wasn't content. Peace eluded him. He'd made bold statements and backed them up with bold actions, but his circumstances hadn't changed, his actions seemed ineffective.

"Everyone was naming and claiming it," Shundrawn says, "but it wasn't working for me. I became increasingly frustrated, confused about my purpose, and uncertain regarding my relationship with God. For years I'd read about everyday people in the Bible that God used to do extraordinary things. But the truth was, I never saw those people as normal or ordinary. While I never doubted that their stories were true, the characters in the Bible simply didn't seem real to me. Then while reading the story of David for what seemed like the hundredth time, God spoke to me. He said I needed to change my perspective. He showed me that my struggle in the area of faith wasn't a lack of faith but of misunderstanding. I had processed the stories and characters of the Bible in the wrong way. I had looked past the human element for a formula and a rational approach to faith. I was searching the scriptures for a step-by-step guide rather than seeing the unique ways that God deals with each person."

For a businessman with a background in finance and formulas, examining God's character in this way had seemed logical. But God desired more from Shundrawn than a business contract. He desired his heart.

"I stopped looking for clues and began to see the personalities, abilities, and situations of the characters. I began to feel their fears, identify with their brokenness, and sense their hopes. I saw them as spiritual persons, not characters in a story. I saw them as special. In essence, I saw them the way God sees them, the way He sees us—as people created in His image."

From this examination, Shundrawn discovered that all people who move forward in faith take the following five steps.

Trust God: He Delights in Your Dreams

"God has something great in store for those who trust in Him, but it's up to us to uncover the treasure He places in our hearts. To those who don't share our faith, the dreams God places in our heart seem ridiculous. But to Him, they are sensible, possible, and part of the expansion of His kingdom. Saul was called by God to be Israel's first king, but Saul didn't trust God. Because of his disbelief and disobedience, he forfeited his position. His absence of faith nullified the promises of God. Saul settled for comfort and succumbed to his fears, and when he did, he forfeited the destiny God intended for him."

> Keep on asking, and you will receive what you ask for.
> Keep on seeking, and you will find. Keep on knocking, and
> the door will be opened to you.
>
> —MATTHEW 7:7, NLT

Know That Problems Point to Possibilities

"Success is born in failure. Insurmountable obstacles force us to seek God. Don't focus on your problems. Instead, focus on the prize. There will always be problems standing between you and your destiny. Saul saw the giant and lost heart, but you don't have to. God is constantly giving us assignments that lie just beyond our human capabilities. He takes us into danger and allows us to stare fear in the face. It is at these pivotal times that we draw on our faith and in doing so, draw closer to God. We are guaranteed victory if we stand on the Word of God, on His promises of protection and provision. Our obstacles are only as big as the space we allow them to occupy in our hearts and minds, so step forward in faith. God always rewards those who pass through the test."

Speak the Word of God

"Despite the criticism of his brother, David continued to speak in faith. The Bible tells us David was repeatedly outspoken in his resolve that a Philistine should not defy the army of the living God. There is a principle at work here. David spoke in faith, and his testimony was made known to the king. When you speak in faith, your testimony is made known to the King. Repeating God's promises and words to Him with reverence and confidence is an act of worship and faith."

Reject Doubt

"When David informed Saul he was willing to fight Goliath, Saul dismissed David's request. He essentially told David that a boy didn't have a chance going up against a proven warrior. Saul's response is typical of what we hear from others when faced with adversity. People project their own fears on us. If they can't envision themselves accomplishing a feat, they assume others will fail, too. Yet, David didn't waver. He refused to let Saul's disbelief upset the condition of his heart." When God has called you to a task, listen to His voice above all others.

> The LORD turned to him and said, "Go in the strength
> you have and save Israel out of Midian's hand. Am I not
> sending you?"
>
> —JUDGES 6:14, NIV

Go in the Strength You Have

"David initially put on the tunic, armor, and sword, but he quickly realized it was unwise to go into battle with weapons he'd never tested. His staff and sling were the weaponry with which he was familiar and the tools that had given him success. His trust in his staff and sling were symbolic of his faith in God. There is an important lesson to be learned. God fully equips us for our destiny before He sends us into the fight. We must have confidence in His promise of protection. As ridiculous as it seemed to others, David was perfectly equipped to claim victory and be comfortable in his uniform. We must have the same confidence that when the opportunity comes, we are already equipped to do what God has called us to do. We should not covet gifts, abilities, and possessions. God has furnished each one of us with exactly what we need to complete our destinies, so fight in the strength He gives you."

Our strength and equipment are revealed in the gifts and abilities God places within us. For Shundrawn, his gift of wisdom allowed him to move past humble beginnings and toward a future filled with hope, possibilities, and Superhuman Performance.

"I've always had this innate ability to make right choices," Shundrawn says. I see this as the gifts of wisdom and discernment. I don't think it's about being smart or knowledgeable. Part of it comes, I think, from just being observant, of having the eyes of God when you look at people and situations. With that talent comes the gift of encouragement. It's just part of my personality. Plus, I've always been one who loves giving to others. Perhaps that's why I became a businessman because as a leader in a position of power, we have the opportunity to impact people in a positive way. But that demands trust. Trust that God will protect us when we act in accordance to His will, that He'll allow our actions to help others, and that our message and actions will ultimately reflect His glory. For me, that's a life lived powered by ridiculous faith."

Gift Wrap

- Don't focus on your problems. Focus on the prize. There will always be problems standing between you and your destiny.

- When you speak in faith, your testimony is made known to the King.

- People project their own fears on us. If they can't envision themselves accomplishing a feat, they assume others will fail, too.

- When God has called you to a task, listen to His voice above all others.

- God has furnished each one of us with exactly what we need to complete our destinies, so fight in the strength He gives you.

Shundrawn's Other Gifts: Leadership, Teaching, and Wisdom

"If any one of you has material possessions and sees a brother or sister in need but has no pity on them, how can the love of God be in you? Dear children, let us not love with words or tongue but with actions and in truth.

—1 JOHN 3:16–18, NIV

CHAPTER 8

FISHERS OF MEN

Fred Fisher: Spending Your Time on People

The harvest is great, but the workers are few. So pray to
the Lord who is in charge of the harvest; ask him to send
more workers into his fields.

—LUKE 10:2, NLT

> **Name:** Frederick E. Fisher
> **Position:** Philanthropist
> **Company:** Retired
> **Gift:** Giving

Calling the Twelve to him, he began to send them out two
by two....Later the apostles gathered around Jesus and
reported to him all they had done and taught.

—MARK 6:7–12, NIV

Trolling in Deep Waters

In the early eighties, Fred Fisher received a call asking if he'd
make a charitable contribution to the University of Florida School

of Accounting. Fred agreed, donating approximately $7 million dollars to the university. What was Fred's motivation? Why give such a large sum?

"Simple," he says. "I was asked. Then, half-joking, I told the President of the university that if I made a gift of that size I'd probably have to go back to work. But that was the situation that presented itself to me. It turned out I actually did go back to work; I became involved in the process for about eight or nine months. And it turned out very well. But, it began because someone asked me to become involved in their dream. That's a lesson I think a lot of people need to learn. You are seldom successful until you invite others into your vision, so ask."

> Fact: Approximately 600 undergraduate and 220 graduate students are enrolled in the Fisher School of Accounting.
>
> Fact: On average, students admitted to Fisher's graduate accounting program score above the 70th percentile on the Graduate Management Aptitude Test (GMAT). Fisher School of Accounting graduates' pass rate on the Certified Public Accountant (CPA) Exam has traditionally been twice as high as the national average. The most recent reported results had the Fisher School at number one for all universities.
>
> Fact: The Fisher School of Accounting is often ranked in the top 10 accounting programs among public universities.

Cast Your Net Wide

"I've said this before, but it's worth repeating: The two most important things on this earth are time and people," Fred says.

"Your success will depend on how you spend your time and with what people. The more you invest your time and treasure in others, the more your life comes into the sunlight.

"This principle of giving begins in the home with your family. Once you've trained yourself to see the needs of those in your home, then you become aware of the many needs in your community, state, or nation. Giving back is key to your success."

Here are a few benefits of giving. Your worth increases. Everyone can give, even if it's just a word of encouragement or smile. Giving reminds you that you are of value and that your actions are valued. Giving liberates. When people release wealth, they testify that they are not slaves to money. Giving builds bridges, expands your social network, and strengthens your ties to the community. And giving blesses both the recipient and donor.

"We have a plethora of organized charitable organizations in our country that are doing exemplary work to fulfill their various missions," Fred says. "But there are so many that need more volunteers. They need people to donate their time and treasures. That's why I encourage business leaders and anyone in a position of influence to use their interests, talents, or resources to knock on and open new doors."

> Believe deep down in your heart that you're destined to do
> great things.
>
> —JOE PATERNO

"For example, years ago we founded Clearwater For Youth. Today it involves over 3,500 kids. The program began as a way to keep kids busy year-round. We started with football. You know, peewee-size and bigger. But because football season only lasts so long, we expanded into baseball, soccer, and basketball. We even had chess for a while. Well, there are literally hundreds of charitable organizations like that around in every community. All you need to do is walk through those doors and offer your time, treasures, and ideas." Look for areas of need and get involved.

Invite Others Into Your Boat

> Ability is what you're capable of doing. Motivation determines what you do. Attitude determines how well you do it.
>
> —LOU HOLTZ

Inspire, invite, and involve others in your vision. "Our Clearwater For Youth program has always been blessed with great people," Fred says. "The truth is, this program is run with a couple hundred volunteers and one paid employee, a former professional ballplayer who's been with us 27 years. In the past we've had legends like Joe DiMaggio and Hank Aaron at our annual fundraiser event. Tommy Lasorda was our master of ceremonies for 12 years. DiMaggio was with us for nine. That's what I mean when I say we're to invest our time in people."

You make a living by what you get. You make a life by what you give. If you want to make an impact in the marketplace, place the people in the market on your portfolio.

> It's not the will to win but the will to prepare to win that makes the difference.
>
> —BEAR BRYANT

Gift Wrap

- You are seldom successful until you invite others into your vision, so ask.

- Giving reminds us we are of value and that our actions are valued.

- Giving liberates.

- Releasing wealth testifies that we are not slaves to money.

- Giving builds bridges, expands your social network and strengthens your ties to the community.

- You make a living by what you get. You make a life by what you give.

Fred's Other Gift: Wisdom

The superior man blames himself. The inferior man blames others.

—DON SHULA

CHAPTER 9

TODAY IS A GREAT DAY FOR A WOW! IMAGE

Lavon Lewis: Your Image is Everything You Do

Do not be misled: Bad company corrupts good character.
—1 CORINTHIANS 15:33, NIV

Name: Lavon Lewis
Position: Founder
Company: Pencilworx Design Group, LLC
Gift: Craftsmanship

You are more than skin color, eyewear, hairstyle, and clothing fashion. You are the product of countless decisions, some made in haste, others planned and proposed with hope, love, and a lifetime commitment. You are the reputation of your actions, the attitude you carry throughout the day, and the feelings you project onto others when you walk into a room. You are your own unique brand.

Every person and business has a brand. You may not think of it in those terms, but whether you're selling bread, chemicals, or accounting services, you project your brand. You are the sum of everything you say and do.

What Does Your Brand Say About You

"Branding is the visual attraction and emotional connection you have with your clients," says Lavon Lewis. "For example, when a client comes into your establishment, you want the location, lobby, and overall atmosphere to welcome them in your absence. You want your employees, company logo, and Web site to reflect the unified identity of your company. Your brand is the culmination of everything you do, your reputation, and the promises you've made. That's why we encourage our clients to make every effort to WOW! their clients. You want to give them a total 360-degree experience that reflects your company's mission and purpose, its values, and moral conduct. This is the essence of branding. If you present yourself properly and give people that WOW! experience, they'll come back. They'll tell others. They'll draw others to you. In short, they become your evangelists."

Seven Steps to Knowing Your Target

Lavon cautions that this holistic branding takes time, focus, and a commitment to evaluating your client's needs. "Research is job one. If you don't know who your clients are, you can't deliver value to them.

"Oftentimes people build Web sites, design logos, or create fliers without really knowing who their target audience is. But the first step is to identify the types of clients you want to attract and serve. Do you want a client in the entertainment industry? If so, at what revenue level? How many employees will this client employ? What is their ethnicity, nationality, culture, and heritage? Is this client gender specific? You want to gather all this information before you begin to build your collateral materials. When you really understand what motivates your clients, you can tailor your brand and deliver value. In other words, the more you focus on your market and the needs of your potential clients, the more successful you will be. So step one is research.

"Step two begins by setting a foundation for your brand," Lavon says. "When I say foundation, I mean your company's color scheme, logo, moniker, and font style. This is the very bottom of your foundation, and these decisions can't be made or changed lightly. Major companies have specific colors tied to their brands. IBM is known as Big Blue. John Deere is known by its yellow and green look. McDonald's is yellow and red. Each of these companies picked their color scheme for a particular purpose.

"A lot of small businesses simply don't understand how color affects the emotions and buying power of the consumer. Red does not mean the same thing in the banking industry as it does in the restaurant business. For example, in food settings, blue spoils your appetite. That's why you don't see a lot of blue used in restaurants, or if you do, it's in small amounts. There is psychology in color, font, and shapes, and you need to know how it works before you launch your brand.

"Consider the color yellow. It invokes images of the sun, suggests life, and delivers the concept of energy and excitement. Think of someone with a 'sunny disposition,' and you begin to see how the McDonald's color theme portrays a friendly and fun atmosphere. Red stimulates hunger. When you put red and yellow together it produces a desire to eat fast, which is why a lot of fast food restaurants use these colors. This is just one of the little factoids we teach in our WOW! Image Seminars. So, in the second step, select colors that attract your perspective clients to your products and services.

"Step three, you need to establish brand awareness," Lavon says. "After you set the foundation, you need to define how you're going to get the word out. Is it through Youtube, Facebook, or Twitter? Or do you simply expect people to find you by your Web site? Will you use print media, fliers, and direct mail? Each of these has its place in your branding strategy. So answer the question: How am I going to let people know I exist?

"Just as importantly, how are you going to promote your brand consistently? Do you have a strategy for long-term media exposure? Do you have a PR campaign? Is everything you do consistent across the board? Is there a totality of purpose and presentation in everything you do? If not, you need to rethink your brand and review your client and target market.

"Step four," Lavon says, "is brand maintenance. After you define your identity, establish your marketing strategy, and launch your brand, you have to maintain that image over time. Often this means you'll have to adapt to new technology. Five years ago no one had heard of Twitter. Now tweets are the latest breaking-news source, in some cases replacing conventional news outlets. So when you think of your brand's communication strategy, ask yourself: Am I tweeting or clucking?

"Step five is storytelling. I can't emphasis this enough. KFC is nothing more than fried chicken, but the Colonel has a story. Papa

Johns is pizza, but they have a story. All great brands use storytelling to convey their messages and attract clients. Without a story, your brand is a commodity. Look at all the media channels and establish ways you're going to get your brand's story out to the public.

"Step six is building brand equity. You want your brand to be worth more at the end of the day than in the morning. Equity, quite simply, is positive word of mouth. Are people saying nice things about your company? Building brand equity doesn't happen overnight. It takes time. It takes effort. It takes focus.

"Finally," Lavon says, "with step seven you have to be willing to adapt, adopt, and advance. Your brand needs to remain flexible to the changes within your industry. Twenty years ago, IBM was a hardware manufacturer selling mainframes to large businesses. Before that they sold typewriters. Over the years they have been seen as a supplier of personal computers, Web servers, software, and calculators. Now they're considered a service company that focuses less on hardware and more on helping companies find business solutions. The IBM brand remains, but their focus continues to shift to meet changes in the marketplace."

Use Your Gifts for Good

Developing a brand strategy is key to the success of any business, but Lavon cautions that we, as individuals, need to be vigilant about our own personal image. This begins with a code of conduct, strong moral character, and a passion for using your gifts for the good of others.

"First," Lavon says, "ask yourself: What would I do for free? When I was in high school, I played the drums and was rated as one of the top five percussionists in the state. Now, I don't play the drums, at least not like I did then. But I do retain that love of music, and it shows in my areas of gifting. I understand beats and rhythm, and this helps me when orchestrating a brand strategy. The things I enjoyed in high school—music, art, even teaching— are the same things I enjoy today, except now I'm using them in my business. I teach seminars, design logos, and create marketing kits. The gifts I enjoyed when I was younger still pay dividends today. So find your area of gifting, and move into a field that will allow you to use those gifts. When you do, you'll find you love what you do.

"Second, develop your gifts. Practice your craft. Read, study, and improve. Become the expert in your field. When you hone your craft, you will raise your own expectations and deliver excellence.

"Lastly, surround yourself with great people who have the gifts you lack. No one can build a business alone. You are going to need help, so recruit individuals gifted in your areas of weakness. Empower them to perform at extraordinary levels. Encourage entrepreneurship within your company, take risks, and accept failure as part of the development process. Not every marketing effort will work out, but the only one guaranteed not to work is the one you never try. So try, learn, and move on.

"The sum of you, as a person, is everything you've ever done and been, and the people you've helped. Find your area of gifting, and use it to improve the lives of those around you. Do that," Lavon says, "and you may find your spiritual gifts launch you into a whole different stratosphere—one reserved for Superhuman Performers."

Gift Wrap

- You are the sum of everything you say and do.

- Research is job one. If you don't know who your clients are, you can't deliver value to them.

- The more you focus on your market and the needs of your potential clients, the more successful you will be.

- Without a story, your brand is a commodity.

- Surround yourself with great people who have the gifts you lack.

Lavon's Other Gift: Teaching

CHAPTER 10

"PLAY" IT FORWARD

Andre Hudson: Physically, Mentally & Spiritually Fit

For physical training is of some value, but godliness has
value for all things, holding promise for both the present
life and the life to come.

—1 TIMOTHY 4:8, NIV

> **Name:** Andre Hudson
> **Position:** Founder
> **Company:** Pro Builder Fitness, Inc.
> **Gift:** Giving

With knees bent and knuckles pressed into the grass, eight
young boys lined up along white chalk lines. The whistle's
quick chirp caused the line to rush forward. As the sound of shoulder pads popping the tackling sled echoed across the practice field,
Andre Hudson looked on. He blew the whistle again and the surge
stopped. "Next time, explode off the ball. Got it?" Helmets nodded.
"Okay, next group. Line up!"

Placing the whistle between his lips, Andre paused. Waiting
was key. The longer he forced them to hold their stance, the

greater the chance a player would jump off sides—not that he was hoping they would. But the repetition of the drill built character and instilled discipline. The boys knew, one false start, and they'd run laps. Two, and they'd run all practice. The legs of the little tykes began to shake with fatigue and anxiety. *Chirp!* Instantly the youngsters lunged, driving the tackling sled backwards. *So small and yet so determined,* Andre thought. *So desperate to improve. If only they'd put the same effort into their studies and spiritual lives.* Another chirp and the blur of churning legs stopped.

"Next! And this time I want to see somebody hit like they mean it!"

Hours later, while the boys knelt in a circle around him, Andre took a few moments to study the boys, looking each one in the eye. "Everybody has a purpose. Everyone has a role. Find yours and execute it flawlessly. Do that, and you'll win. Not just in sports but in life, too. Understood?"

A timid hand went up. "Coach?"

"Yeah, son?"

"What's your role?"

"To make sure you can tackle the guy with the ball and whatever else life throws at you. Now, line up, again."

Mentally Tough

As founder of Pro Builder Fitness, Andre Hudson knows what it's like to line up in front of a giant opponent and feel the heat of his breath in his own face mask.

"Several years ago I was having some difficulties, both personally and professionally," Andre says. "I owned a fitness gym, but family issues and a few other things had set me back. It was a tough period for me, and I couldn't decide whether to shut it down or keep going. The situation had gotten so bad, all I could do was turn it over to God. Around that time I remembered a story in the Bible where another man was stuck and unable to see any way out of his problems. Abraham was ready to sacrifice the thing he loved most, his son Isaac. He'd reached the point where he just had to trust God to take care of things even though he couldn't see how.

"Right about that time, figuratively speaking, God sent a ram into the bushes to save me.

He brought this man into my life, Dexter Gabboard. Dexter sat me down and together we just brainstormed about my situation, tossed out ideas, kicked around names for my business, and lo and behold, he blurts out, 'Pro Builder Fitness,' and 'Lives Under Construction.' He's the one who suggested I take the concept of physical fitness and match it with spiritual training. For two straight days, we met at his house, and I wrote down everything he said. What God had done, without me realizing it, was lead a man into my life who could speak his vision to me and help me recreate my businesses with God at the center."

> The main purpose of money is not to meet needs but first to accomplish God's purposes on earth.
> —PASTOR SUNDAY ADELAJA

Physically Fit

Andre believes God will oftentimes illuminate a physical weakness or affliction in order to shine His light on a spiritual flaw that needs attention.

"I understood how to train the body. That was my passion. I'd been helping people get physically fit for years. But I really hadn't thought of it as a ministry. Then not long after my meeting with Dexter, he died in a freak accident. But because of the way he'd helped me see the potential to serve God in the thing I love, I wanted to give back, both to God and to those around me. So I began looking for ways I could help other young men and women reach their physical and spiritual potential.

"I've always enjoyed working with youth. I especially like to catch them when they're around the age of seven or eight. If you can build a solid foundation under them, then they have a greater chance of making it to the next level. That's why, whenever I get a group of young kids together, I always have the smaller ones watch the bigger ones. It helps for the little guys to see the different footwork routines by guys who've already been through the drills. And I'm quick to remind them that it's the same in life. I tell them that one day young eyes will be watching them, so they need to make sure they have the technique nailed or else they might lead the next group astray. The problem I found, though, as I tried to reach out to younger kids, was that a lot of them couldn't afford the kind of professional training I offered. They wanted to improve their core strength and speed, their quickness and agility, but most couldn't afford it."

Spiritually Humble

Because Andre had a heart for helping, he decided to set up a scholarship program for young kids that would allow them to take advantage of his training.

"I think this is one of the keys to developing your spiritual gift. You have to give back, even when it costs you. You need to remember that the gift is God's, not yours. For me, giving has always been second nature. I guess you could say I was blessed with the gift of giving early in my life. My grandmother knew I had it and would often point it out to me. I was always the giver, no matter what was going on in my life. Even when I was a kid and running around at night in places I shouldn't have been, I'd always come back to check on my siblings and take care of them. That was just something I've always done. So, having a willingness to give back will help others help you grow your gift.

> We were commanded to be fruitful. Without money, our
> ability to bear kingdom fruit is minimal.
> —PASTOR SUNDAY ADELAJA

"But just because you're willing to help others without any thought of monetary reward doesn't mean your work isn't valuable. And that was one of the things I wanted the kids who came to my gym to understand. I wanted them to know the value of the training they were receiving and respect it. And I wanted them to be held accountable.

"When we'd get together, I'd tell them, 'First, you're going to meet me on the field at a specific time, not just sometime. We'll pick a time that works for both of us.' Second, I told them, 'I expect you to be here on time, not a little or lot afterwards.' Third, 'You're gonna do community service work.' Again, I wanted them to understand the importance of giving back, of 'playing' it forward. This idea of playing forward is huge because it allows the blessings we've received to flow to others. Fourth, I told them, 'You are going to bring your report card. If you're not doing well in school, we'll work on that, too.' I want my kids to understand that physical training will only carry them so far. You have to train your mind, body, and soul to perform at a superhuman level. Finally, I explained that I expected them to be respectful. I'd tell them, 'If you've got a doctor's appointment that requires you to miss our appointment or if you have to stay at school, let me know beforehand. Don't just pop up later and say, 'Oh, I decided to stay home.' That's not gonna cut it because ultimately we're all accountable to someone, a boss, a spouse, parents, teachers, God.

"He calls us to love Him with all our strength, all our heart, body, and soul. And we can't do that if we're mentally, physically, and spiritually lazy. So my advice to kids and adults is the same. Get in shape—God shaped. And then get busy giving back."

> The best stewardship of all is to raise up others to be successful.
>
> —PASTOR SUNDAY ADELAJA

Gift Wrap

- Playing forward is huge because it allows the blessings we've received to flow to others.

- Get in shape—God shaped. And then get busy giving back.

Andre's Other Gift: Encouragement

CHAPTER 11

GROWING WEALTH GOD'S WAY

William R. Patterson: Making Your Pennies Prosper

Jesus took the five loaves and two fish, looked up toward heaven, and blessed them. Then, breaking the loaves into pieces, he kept giving the bread to the disciples so they could distribute it to the people. He also divided the fish for everyone to share. They all ate as much as they wanted, 43 and afterward, the disciples picked up twelve baskets of leftover bread and fish. A total of 5,000 men and their families were fed from those loaves!

—MARK 6:41–44, NLT

> Name: William R. Patterson
> Position: Chairman & CEO
> Company: The Baron Solution Group
> Gift: Knowledge

William Patterson's mother often shaped his thinking when he was a young boy through the stories they read together. One day she sat William down to read him a story that would forever influence his life. She walked over to the bookshelf, and after a moment of searching, pulled out a thin colorful book. Mrs. Patterson sat down next to William and began to read him the story of a young boy from Lima, Peru who was asked to go to the market to buy food for his family. William listened intently as his mom read, imagining he was the little boy in the story. In his mind, William was traveling down the dusty road on the way to market. Lions crouched near the ditch, their amber manes kissed by the sun and bleached like the color of the weeds in which they hid. Jungle sounds crowded around him. The story held the promise of danger and great adventure. Mrs. Patterson turned the page and continued reading.

The boy in the story hesitated at the edge of the village, unsure of which vendor to approach first. Ahead stood a large round butcher with his meat clever. Chickens hung by their feet, their necks, limp. As the boy jingled the coins in his pocket, William felt their heaviness and envisioned the soggy bills moist with the boy's sweat.

Just then a young girl appeared on the page. In the story, she darted up to the boy, pleading for his help. "Please! My family, we are starving. Won't you give me some money?" William sensed the boy's dilemma. Should he buy food for his family or help the young girl? His mom turned the page and William saw the scowl on the mother's face and knew the boy was in trouble.

"You gave away *all* our grocery money!" the mother yelled.

"She was hungry. You should have seen her," said the boy.

"Yes, but now how will we eat?"

"Let me try again. I will be more careful this time."

The mother in the story sent her son to town again, replenishing his pockets with money. Again he met hungry faces. This time he met a family he was tempted to help, but then he remembered how angry his mother had been. He counted the money in his pockets and went to the vendors. Pointing to the hungry family, the boy negotiated with the street merchants, asking them to sell him food at a discounted price. They agreed. The boy provided for both his family and theirs. From then on, when it was time to go to the village, the mother sent the boy because he always bought enough for them and enough for others.

"That book, *The Boy Who Made His Pennies Go A Long Way,* taught me a great lesson," says William Patterson. "I think I was around six when my mom read that book to me. But what I remember is this: Use your talents and abilities to help others, but do it in a way that you do not make the other person's burden your own. By not depleting your resources in service to another person, you'll be able to help not only them but numerous others. Just as Jesus fed many with what appeared to be little, so too must each person connect with their own divine nature to see a way when there appears to be none."

Entrusted With a Dream

Though William was trained as an electrical engineer, he found his passion lay in business and finance. He quickly discovered that the closer you got to the bottom line, the more impact and influence you could have in a company. By the late nineties, William had worked on Wall Street and for a number of top information technology and consulting firms. His next step was to branch out and start his own financial holding company.

"When I first started my career, my goal was to become Chief Executive Officer of a Fortune 100 company. Well, you know how a lot of kids today say they want to become professional basketball players, and people look at them like they're delusional because the odds are stacked against them. In fact, the odds are so overwhelming that you have a better chance of getting struck by lightning than making it to the NBA. One in 750,000 people gets hit by lightning. One in a million becomes a pro basketball player. So when I considered the odds of an African American male becoming the CEO of a Fortune 100 company, I knew I was going to have an even tougher road. With this in mind, I had a decision to make. I could either take my chances on being promoted to the top in corporate America or make my own way as an entrepreneur. I chose the latter."

Fortunately William knew the path to the top is best traversed with the help of others, so he sought the support of great mentors, people like Christopher J. Williams, the 41-year-old CEO and president of Williams Capital Group L.P., and Bob Johnson, founder of Black Entertainment Television.

"With the support of these men and top advisors, I was able to build a number of successful companies," William says. "As a result, in 2005, I, along with Vicky Therese Davis and D. Marques Patton, wrote the book *The Baron Son* to share insights that would help others reach their financial and entrepreneurial dreams faster. The book was an allegorical tale designed as an ethical roadmap to wealth, power, and success. From there, we created The Baron Solution Group, a coaching and consulting firm that helps individuals and organizations grow their income and improve profitability by creating greater value for others."

The Five Wealth Principles

In his book *The Baron Son*, William and his co-authors reveal a number of timeless wealth-building principles. The book illustrates how individuals can tap into their passion, obtain support from others, and rapidly improve their financial circumstances no matter where they are starting from.

"No one will ever care as much about your financial success as you do," says William. "You can hire professional advisors to assist you with planning and financial decision making, but ultimately you are responsible for your financial future. The first thing people need to understand when it comes to building wealth is that not all sources of income are created equal. Some sources of income bear less fruit and force you to work harder than others.

"Unfortunately, in school we're taught to strive for earned income which is not designed to create financial independence. With our approach, The Baron Solution, we identify the various types of income, assets, and strategies that will help or hinder one's ability to build wealth quickly."

Earned Income

"Earned income depends on your physical labor. It requires you to exchange your time for money. With this type of income, the amount of money you can make is inherently limited because there is only a finite amount of time that a person is able to work. Financial freedom is very difficult to obtain with earned income because if you stop working or you lose your job, your income also stops. That's why one of the first things we encourage people to do is to move from earned income to more passive and residual income streams."

Passive & Residual Income

"Passive and residual income streams," William says, "are ideal for achieving financial independence because they don't require you to trade your time for money on an ongoing basis. You can build wealth by taking a one-time action or creating a product or service, one that will have a recurring income stream. Sources of passive income include royalties from intellectual property such as inventions, books, and music. Rental income is another great example of passive income. You may have to invest time and capital in the property, but you don't need to be present to earn income. Residual income streams can be created from things like network marketing and direct sales programs. Lately, network marketing has earned a bad reputation, but the principle remains sound: sell a product or service once and reap a recurring income. Passive and residual income streams allow you to own your time so that you don't have to work for money. They give you the freedom to focus on your million-dollar idea, the things you're most passionate about, and your divine purpose."

Create Value

"Wealth begins to flow when you create value for others and are consistent with your divine purpose," Williams says. "I learned early on that value was the greatest attracting force of money in the world. A lot of people miss this one. They think just because they show up, employers will want to pay them more, or, in the case of executives and entrepreneurs, customers will automatically want to buy their companies' products and services. However, the most successful individuals are always asking themselves, 'How can I deliver greater value to my organization, customers, clients, and partners?' They know that the fastest way to achieve success is to increase the value that they deliver to others.

"Financial success is multiplied even further when people raise their value using one or more of the three major wealth-building vehicles: entrepreneurship, real estate, and the stock market. Wealth building can be accelerated using these vehicles because they provide a person with financial leverage, and there is no limit to the amount of money one can make. In the entrepreneurship arena, you can look at people like Bill Gates. He's created value for computer users by helping people to do things better, faster, and cheaper through software. In the process, he has created billions of dollars in wealth for shareholders. When it comes to real estate, you have people like Donald Trump who take underdeveloped land and make improvements to that land to increase its value. In the stock market, you have Warren Buffett who finds companies that are underpriced, buys them, and then waits for the market to recognize their true value. To be consistent with your divine purpose, it is important to ask yourself everyday, 'Is this the greatest value and benefit that I can deliver to the world?'"

Deliver Solutions

"Your passion and your problems," William says, "are two of the most powerful driving forces that you can quickly turn into a viable new business or a new profit center for an existing business. If you have ever done anything successfully in your life that you are also passionate about, you can turn that into a viable business.

For those few individuals who claim to possess no marketable skills or passion, they are in luck too. You can always turn your problems into a viable business as well. If you have a particular issue, it is very likely that there are at least thousands of other people or organizations that have the same dilemma. The key to turning your problems into profits is choosing the right problem that people are willing to pay to have solved. Since everyone has problems, everyone has the potential to become a successful entrepreneur. The more problems you solve and the bigger they are, the greater your opportunities and income."

William offers this example of someone who saw a problem and found a solution. "A few years ago, a client named Sasha Ottey came to us after being diagnosed with Polycystic Ovarian Syndrome. PCOS is an endocrine and metabolic disorder that is estimated to affect one in 10 women of childbearing age. It is the leading cause of infertility in women and a precursor for other serious conditions including obesity and endometrial cancer. Women with PCOS also constitute the largest group of women at risk for developing cardiovascular disease and type 2 diabetes. After her diagnosis, Sasha was faced with a defining moment in her life. She could give up or fight. She was determined to overcome PCOS, but after a lot of time searching, she struggled to find adequate support and resources for her condition. She knew that if she was having a difficult time finding answers, other women were too. So, Sasha decided to leave her full-time job as a microbiologist to create a nonprofit organization called PCOS Challenge to help make a difference in the lives of millions of women with Polycystic Ovarian Syndrome. The Baron Solution Group helped Sasha launch her nonprofit organization, attract funding, and develop a television show and radio show to bring greater awareness about PCOS. In just over a year, PCOS Challenge has grown to over 7,000 members worldwide.

"This is a great example of how one can turn a problem into an opportunity to help others. And in doing so, create wealth in every sense of the word. Sometimes the things that challenge us are merely the catalysts to help us use our spiritual gifts more fully and to realize our divine callings."

Leveraging OPE: Other People's Everything

"The fourth way to rapidly increase your income and build wealth," William says, "is to leverage other people's time, money, resources, networks, skills, and credibility. We call this employing intelligent leverage. I always say there is no shortage of opportunity, only a shortage of insight because any situation of lack can be solved through a partnership. You'll find that you can always get people to help you if you first determine the value and benefit that you can bring to the other person or organization. Many people struggle to build wealth because they attempt to do too much alone. Out of fear, habit, overconfidence, or convenience, they choose to do everything themselves even when securing help from others would give them 10 to 100 times greater results. In working alone, they diminish their spiritual gifts and limit the impact they can have in the world.

"The key to leveraging OPE is to make it easy for other people to help you. You can significantly increase your income, credibility, and odds for long-term success by offering turnkey solutions. If you present well thought-out, ready-made, and proven solutions that require little to no work for your mentors, colleagues, and joint-venture partners, you can dramatically increase your buy-in, support, sales, customer retention, and referrals. Profit lies in reducing the amount of work that others must do to receive the benefit that your idea has to offer."

Diversified Income

"The fifth way to grow wealth is to diversify your income and expand into new markets," William says. "When you intelligently expand into untapped markets, your chances of success increase exponentially, providing a buffer should the economy suffer around you. It follows the old adage, *Don't put all you eggs in one basket.*

"A lot of people wake up and say, 'Wow, the economy is tough.' And for some it is. But consider the person in Poland who has never heard of your product or service. Think about acquiring customers in emerging markets, like India and China. When you open your mind to possibilities beyond your current sphere of influence and business dealings, you immediately see new growth opportunities. This insight is revealed in *The Baron Son* when the following question is asked of the story's protagonist by a potential investor to test his will, 'How long will you continue to market and promote your products?' The Baron replied, 'Until there is no person walking the earth who does not know my name.' To avoid the impact of an economic downturn, people should seek the guidance of experts and investigate expanding their efforts nationally and internationally. The greatest ideas and spiritual gifts have no borders."

William reminds his clients often of that story from his childhood, the one about the boy whose creative thinking and partnerships enabled him to solve larger problems despite his own limited resources. When you connect with your divine nature and Godly purpose, doors will open. Know that every obstacle you encounter is ultimately for your benefit. So learn from each circumstance because the insights and experience you gain will provide a key that will open a door of opportunity for you later.

Gift Wrap:

- Your passion and your problems are two of the most powerful driving forces that you can quickly turn into a viable new business or a new profit center for an existing business.

- Passive and residual income streams are ideal for achieving financial independence because they don't require you to trade your time for money on an ongoing basis.

- Know that every obstacle you encounter is ultimately for your benefit. So learn from each circumstance because the insights and experience you gain will provide a key that will open a door of opportunity for you later.

William's Other Gifts: Encouragement and Leadership

CHAPTER 12

WHAT'S YOUR STORY?

Eddie Jones: Writing to Make Your Joy Complete

In the beginning was the Word, and the Word was with
God, and the Word was God.
—JOHN 1:1, HOLMAN CHRISTIAN STANDARD BIBLE

> Name: Eddie Jones
> Position: Writer, Speaker & Coach
> Company: WritersCoach.us
> Gift: Writing

Eddie pulled into the campground and parked near the bathhouse. He opened the rear hatch, and carried the ground tarp,
tent, and lantern to the campsite. A cool northeast wind blew across
the field, bringing the smell of rain. Nearby, a portable generator
parked next to an RV kicked on. Unfolding the tent, he hooked the
corners in place, thinking as he did, of how stupid he looked. *What
fool drives five hours to a writers' conference and camps in a state park,*
he wondered.

Almost two years earlier, on the exact date, Eddie had lost his job. Oh, he knew where it was. His job as Web developer for IBM was in Bangalore, India, and it wasn't coming back, so he'd spent the last of his birthday money on the conference fee. All he had left was a dream, his book manuscript, and a faint whisper from God that he was on the right path. Now that path had led him to a cold campsite. Assembling the plastic poles, he snapped them in place, lifting the tent from the ground just as the first drops of rain hit.

By the time he'd loaded his gear in the tent, his jeans and sweatshirt were soaked. He crawled inside and curled himself around the lantern. Opening his Bible, he read the passage from that morning's devotion. "The Lord has done great things for us. We are filled with joy." (Psalm 126:3) On the ruled lines of his prayer journal, he'd written "But the seed on good soil stands for those with a noble and good heart, who hear the word, retain it, and, by persevering, produce a crop." (Luke 8:15) Was his heart noble and good? Had he retained God's word? Was his dream, the writing, and this trip perseverance or stupidity?

Clicking off the lantern, Eddie lay on the hard ground, listening to the sound of the rain, recalling the words of his last manager. "Where do you see yourself in five years?" Without thinking, he'd blurted out, "Sailing around the Caribbean while writing a bestselling novel and surfing reef breaks."

"All kidding aside," his manager had said. "Where do you see yourself within this company?"

That was just it. Eddie didn't see himself in that company—or any other company. And now, looking back, he understood why. God's plans for his life were about to change. He'd sensed the shift without understanding the consequences of the tremors. When he awoke the next morning, his sleeping bag was wet. He showered, slipped on a pair of clean khakis, dress shirt, and sweater vest, and drove to the conference. The first class left him depressed. The agent, a woman who'd spent over twenty years in the book publishing industry, offered little hope. "Most writers fail to get an agent," she had explained.

"Few novels reach an editor's desk. Even if your book is selected for publication, the royalties are abysmal," she'd added. "Most writers never make more than their advance which can be as little as three thousand dollars."

He hoped to take a walk around campus before dinner, but cold rain pelted the windows of the cafeteria. He worried about his tent, wishing now that he'd put his duffle bag in the car. Strolling into the dining room, he took a seat at a table with other writers. While they chatted about their manuscripts, he re-read a verse from his prayer journal, one he'd added days earlier. "Our mouths were filled with laughter, our tongues with songs of joy. Then it was said among the nations, 'The Lord has done great things for them.'" (Psalm 126:2–3)

Great things? Songs of joy? Laughter? All he felt was a sense of failure. He'd followed his dream, taken the bold step of faith, and announced to his family that he was going to pursue his dream of writing. Now look at him. He couldn't even afford a motel room. When the dishes were cleared, the keynote speaker offered a few words of encouragement. "Don't write to be published," he said. "Write because you have to. Write because God has placed a message on your heart that only you can deliver. Write because to do anything else defiles who you are and is an insult to the God who created you."

Listening to the words, Eddie felt convicted. He thought the gift was for him. Had he put too much emphasis on winning the approval of others? Hadn't he signed up to write for God alone? Maybe this was success, just doing the thing you love regardless of the applause from others.

The conference director stepped to the podium and began to hand out awards for poetry, short stories, and articles. When they reached the novel category, the room fell silent. The third and second place winners rushed forward, stood for their pictures, and retuned to their seats. Eddie picked at a piece of chocolate cake. The conference director leaned toward the mic and said, "And in the category of unpublished novels, our first place winner is Eddie Jones."

Eddie's fork hit the plate. The room shrank. He saw the others clapping, motioning for him to go up front. When he reached the podium, he stared at the certificate for several seconds before his eyes noticed the check clipped to it—$1,000.

In his car on the way back to his campsite, he wept. He'd heard God's voice calling him to write, but he'd never really believed that God would bless him. "Take up your cross and suffer." Wasn't that the suffering servant's grim Gospel? Why should he expect good news, laughter, and joy from God? And yet, God had honored him.

As Eddie neared the bathhouse, his headlights illuminated the crumpled heap of his tent. Wind had snapped a pole. His sleeping bag and clothes were soaked. But he didn't mind. The rain couldn't wash away the joy he felt. Stuffing it all into the trunk of his car, he crawled behind the wheel and looked at the winning manuscript sitting on the passenger's seat and the check beside it.

"Come on, book," Eddie said. "We got an upgrade. We're sleeping in God's Kingdom tonight."

Eddie's journey from toilet paper salesman to writer spanned nearly four decades, taking him from International Paper to IBM. Along the way, he constantly felt that he was succeeding from a position of weakness, that his accomplishments, while notable, were at odds with his true calling.

The Introduction

"I've always been drawn to words. As a kid, I read *Tom Sawyer* every summer. The story became so familiar that I could write a book report on the novel from memory, which I did almost every year. The notion that Tom was confined to a life ill-suited to his personality resonated within me. I never wanted to be Huck Finn. Huck was too brash and uncultured. But Tom, now there was a boy who understood that his life had a purpose and there was more to it than following the rules set down by his aunt, preacher, and teachers."

Motivation

"I'd go off into the woods and build forts and ride my bike miles from my house, all the while making up stories in my head where I was a pirate or great explorer discovering a new land. When I reached high school, I weaseled my way onto the school newspaper. I sold ads, mostly, but occasionally they'd let me write an article."

Begin the Hero's Quest

"Then, the last semester of my senior year in high school, I mentioned to my English teacher that I was planning to go to college. 'You? In college?' she said. 'You're not college material.' I told her I was going anyway, that I had to. She said if I was serious, she'd help get me ready but it would take a lot of work."

Change the Hero's Direction

"I passed Mrs. Pollard's English class with a C—or maybe a D," Eddie says. "She was right. I wasn't college material. My college application was rejected. But, after meeting with an admissions officer and asking if they could find a spot for me, N.C. State invited me to enroll in their college of industrial arts (It helped that I wore the State colors to my interview: A white shirt, red tie, and a pair of red and white polyester pants my mom had made). Of course, I didn't know anything about how to fix stuff; I couldn't even repair my lawn mower. So, I never took the first industrial arts course."

Challenge the Hero With Problems

"Again, my high school English teacher proved right. I flunked freshman English twice before passing with a D on the third try. I landed a job with *The Technician*, State's newspaper, and wrote for them all four years. I kept taking journalism classes to improve my reporting skills. I was a lousy grammarian. Still am. But the classes were fun. I think that's the first time I sensed that I was called to write. What was work for others was fun to me, even though I struggled. I'd say that's one of the keys to finding your spiritual gifts. What's hard but fun can be a pointer to your passion and purpose."

Status Change

"Four years later," Eddie says, "I graduated from State with a degree in English. I decided not to go into journalism, though, because reporters didn't make jack. Instead, I took a construction job making twice what my friends were making at the small newspapers. Then that fall, while I was pouring cement, a guy named Shaky, who drank his lunch, said, 'How come you never went to college?' Told him I had. 'Flunked out?' he asked. I explained that I'd graduated that spring and was working construction 'cause it paid better than reporting. He stopped and stared at me. 'You graduated from college and you doing this?' he said. 'Dang, man. You ain't never gonna 'mount to nothing.' His words scared me. Up until that point, I just figured things would work out. You go to college, get a degree, and a good job finds you. But he made me realize you have to make your own breaks if you want to get ahead. You can't just sit back and wait for folks to find you."

Give the Hero Tougher Problems

"A month later I took a job as a sales trainee for a paper company," Eddie says. "Worked my way into a territory, did well for a while, then switched to a competitor. Eventually, I became one of their top salesmen. Then the company—a family-run business— sold out to International Paper. I'd been through that drill with my previous employer, so I knew how it would end—staff reductions, cut commissions, and poor service. Any time a big firm takes over, the customers suffer because, to the big guys, it's all about the shareholder price and short-term profits. Service, quality, and reputation are the casualties of consolidation. Sure enough, after a few years, we stopped servicing about half of my accounts. I was desperate to find new work so I taught myself how to build Web pages and landed a job at IBM."

Let the Hero Suffer Maximum Angst

"I spent seven years working for IBM before they went through another re-org and moved my unit off-shore. I could've stayed, doing project management work, but my heart wasn't in it. One thing I've learned about God's leading is when the Spirit leaves, it's time to move on. So, I took their severance package and went home to see where God would lead me next."

Offer the Hero a Transition

"During all my jobs, I continued to write for magazines. Even wrote a couple of nonfiction books. So, when a friend invited me to go with him to a writers' conference, I figured, *why not?* Had nothing else to do. During the opening session, the keynote speaker said, 'If God has called you to write, then write. You may not ever get published. You may not ever make any money from anything you write. But, if God has called you to write, then write.

"When I left that auditorium, I went back to my room and cried because I knew God was speaking to me. I said, 'Lord, I'm tired of chasing the next job so, if you call, I'll do whatever you ask.' I figured whatever job He gave me was better than what I could come up with."

Change the Hero's Direction Again

"For the next few years," Eddie says, "I ran my own Web business. Then, a few years ago, I heard God whisper, 'ChristianDevotions.com.' Since I knew how to register domains, I figured God wanted me to register that one. Before I could get to my desk, though, I forgot. This went on for a few weeks, with God reminding me to register that domain and me forgetting. When I finally did remember, I learned the dot com domain was taken, but dot US was not, so I registered ChristianDevotions.US."

Give the Hero New Hope

"A few months later, I got an e-mail from a girl I'd met at the writers' conference. She'd been at the conference the year I'd heard God speaking through the keynote address. Because of his words, she'd written a devotion every day for three years. She said she'd love to write for my Web site, but then added, 'You'll have to write, too. It can't just be me.' Now, each week I write a devotion with Cindy Sproles called, 'He Said, She Said.'"

Hero Wins or Loses What He's After

"Today, we have over 200 writers working for Christian Devotions Ministry. Our e-mail subscriber list reaches over 10,000 readers each week, and our Web site gets visits from people throughout the world. We have a Spanish-language site and a loyal following of Cuban readers who can only get the devotions via e-mail. Last year, we launched a children's site called DevoKids.com. We host two radio shows each week and next year we'll host our first DevoFest, a kid-centered writing, acting, broadcasting, and script-writing event for young people ages 7–17. We also have a new teen site called iBeGat.com edited and run by teens."

Tie Up Loose Ends

"We're now an official 501(c)(3) nonprofit organization," Eddie says, "and we've done it all without borrowing any money. Any time we need money, we just ask God, present the needs, and trust Him for the answer. And it's all because when God called, other people and I said, 'yes.' Now my question to every one I meet is 'What's your story?' And by that I mean, why aren't you following God's voice on the journey to which He's called you? If we'll only follow His voice, there's no limit to how far He can take us."

Gift Wrap

- Don't write to be published. Write because you have to. Write because God has placed a message on your heart that only you can deliver. Write because to do anything else defiles who you are and is an insult to the God who created you.

- You have to make your own breaks if you want to get ahead. You can't just sit back and wait for folks to find you.

- What's your story? And by that I mean, why aren't you following God's voice on the journey to which He's called you? If we'll only follow His voice, there's no limit to how far He can take us.

Eddie's Other Gifts: Teaching and Faith

MUSIC

Music is the gift that allows people to inspire others and provide comfort to them through instrumental music, singing, or dancing. People with this gift also use it to share personal testimonies and express faith so others may benefit.

People with this gift:

- Sing or play a musical instrument well and enjoy it.

- Have special joy singing praises to God, either alone or with other people.

- Are confident that their musical ability will be of benefit to other people with whom they come in contact.

- See that their singing or instrument playing is a spiritual encouragement for others.

PUSH YOUR DREAMS AS IF THEY WERE AS LIGHT AS A FEATHER

Abraham McDonald: From Obscurity to Oprah

Let the word of Christ dwell in you richly as you teach
and admonish one another with all wisdom, and as you
sing psalms, hymns and spiritual songs with gratitude in
your hearts to God.

—COLOSSIANS 3:16, NIV

> **Name:** Abraham McDonald
> **Position:** Musical Performer
> **Company:** Abraham McDonald, Inc.
> **Gift:** Music

Abraham McDonald shifted in his chair and looked into the camera, welcoming fans into his hotel room. "Good Morning, YouTube. It's 5:52 A.M., L.A. time, but it's a little later here in

Chicago. I'm getting ready to go down to the studio to work on the song I'll be performing Thursday."

Thursday. The final night of "Oprah's 1st Karaoke Challenge." The three finalists have spent days preparing for the last show. Abraham's early morning shout-out on YouTube is part of his appeal to fans, a way of garnering support and influence with the judges. But his voice is the real draw. In the previous weeks he wowed the world with his singing. Now, as his final performance draws near, he seems humbled by the experience.

He looks away and drops his head. Abraham is a large man and now almost larger than life as the rush of fame overwhelms him. Leaning forward in his chair, he speaks into the portable video monitor, appearing anxious and self-conscious, as if finally coming to grips with the fact that his life is about to change in a large way.

Abraham pulls back the curtain and looks across the Chicago skyline. In some ways, this simple gesture mirrors his faith, as though God is pulling away a veil and allowing Abraham to see the land to which he is heading. He opens his mouth to speak, then pauses, as if searching for just the right words to describe how he's feeling on the edge of his own promised land.

"I can't say I've prepared my entire life for this moment, but I thank God that He's positioned me for this. Now, I can receive His gift of love, His favor."

The day of the finals, Abraham arrives at Harpo Studios, home of the *Oprah Winfrey Show*. Harpo (Oprah spelled backward) is the only studio complex in the world owned by an African American woman. Purchased in 1988, this former armory is now a state-of-the-art production facility—and Abraham's launching platform.

For the final event, Oprah has added a new panel of celebrity judges: Diane Warren, L.A. Reid, and David Foster. She's also had the finalists practice with vocal coach Ken Hicks. Backstage, the three contestants draw numbered microphones indicating the order in which they'll perform. Abraham will go first. He paces during the commercial break, taking deep breaths, praying for strength, asking for peace. Then, with the audience cheering on cue, Oprah introduces the first contestant.

"Performing Oleta Adams' hit song, *Get Here,* please welcome finalist number one, Abraham McDonald!"

The camera zooms in on Abraham as he begins, "You can reach me by railway...." For the next few moments, he belts out the words, his face contorting, eyes wide. He channels the song's energy to the audience. The camera cuts to the judges. David Foster's head is bowed, his hand shielding his face. Another shot shows Abraham's sister, Breeze, swaying to the music, mouthing the words. Oprah is leaning forward in her chair and seems to be blown away by the performance. The crowd stands. Even watching on TV, you can feel the excitement and the spirit of the man.

When the song ends, Oprah walks on stage, letting slip a small yelp. Regardless of the judges' final decision, one thing is clear: God has gifted Abraham McDonald with an incredible ability. How he uses that gift could possibly define his legacy.

RECOGNIZE THE WEIGHT OF GOD'S FAVOR

"I think everyone has a gift," Abraham says, months after his *Oprah* performance. "Music is mine. I actually knew around the age of ten that I could sing. We used to sing around the neighborhood, and I could tell that I sounded just a little better than my sister and brothers. Not a lot, but a little. It wasn't until the season I'm in now, though, that I recognized what God wants me to do with the gift. When you recognize the weight of His favor, when you know how you are to use your gift, then you don't want to play around with it. That's why I'm really thoughtful about what I choose to sing and how I choose to sing it.

"For me, singing is like fresh rain. It cleanses your mind, breaks the yoke. Even if you're not in the best of tone, singing enables you to go into a place with your King, your Father. If the worship is sincere, if it's true, if it's honest, then you'll definitely get to His seat."

There is a sense of deep gratitude as this 32-year-old singer reflects on how far he's come. "I know what rough feels like. I know what sad looks like. And I know what hurt is, but God came to me. He healed me."

For years, Abraham didn't like where he was. He felt out of place, discouraged, and uneasy with his gift of music. "I got to a point where I was so frustrated, I began to abuse the energy around me. When you aren't happy you start saying stuff to people like you're crazy. You don't really care how it comes out of your mouth. There's no filter. And the filter isn't even about not hurting someone's feelings. The filter is more about representing who you serve.

I knew that my mantra had become one of just wanting to be of service. But I wasn't happy.

"I remember my sister coming into my room one day and saying, 'You don't celebrate you.' I didn't even know what that meant. So she said, 'When you talk about someone else, your face lights up. You're talking about them as if you don't believe you're worthy of the same.'

"You see," Abraham says, "I'd come to believe that service work meant that you didn't get to have a say in what you did or how you accomplished it. You didn't get to pat yourself on the back. But I think for those of us in the ministry, it's very important to recognize that you cannot celebrate someone else until you celebrate yourself. And that ultimately means looking in the mirror daily and celebrating the river that's flowing in you. That's God. If you're tapped into your life source, the energy, the love energy of God, if you're looking at yourself daily and loving yourself more because you're loving Him more, then in most cases you'll supersede the negativity that tries to weigh you down. You'll begin to see yourself colorful again.

"I was living a very black and white kind of life. It wasn't until God began using people around me to confront that brokenness that I was forced to deal with those wounds. The best medicine came from a letter my mom gave me. I wanted to know why my dad left, so one day while I was gone she stuffed a letter in my Bible. It read, 'Son, I will tell you whatever it is you want to know. Good, bad, ugly, and indifferent. However, don't allow your feelings to be a reason you don't become who God made you to be.'

"Right then," Abraham says, "I knew that I needed to start accessing my feelings. No one wants to see a grown man running around crying all the time, but there is a prayer closet where we can go and cry out to our Father. If we get into a position where we give ourselves over and release to His energy flow, then we can go outside of ourselves and forgive those who've hurt us. For me that was key. Getting over the hurt. Learning to forgive."

GET READY & BE READY

Abraham's sister, Breeze, led him to the Chester Washington Golf Course to audition for the L.A. County Fair Karaoke competition. The prize was $1,000, just enough to fix his car. Not only did he win male vocalist of the year at the L.A. County Fair, but a representative of the *Oprah Winfrey Show*, in search of the country's best karaoke singer, told Abraham he might get a phone call. But he didn't—at least, not right away.

Thirty days passed. Nothing. Finally, someone phoned from Harpo Studios asking him to audition again. He received a Fed-Ex package with a Skype kit inside, hooked up the equipment, and began preparing for his audition.

The next morning, Abraham dialed into the show, assuming he and a few judges would be on the call while he performed. Then Oprah appeared. She told him that not only was he streaming live but that he had already reached the semi-final round. A short time later, he received a plane reservation in his e-mail. Abraham was on his way to Chicago and Harpo Studios.

So how did Abraham McDonald come to realize he had not just a gift but a calling? "One, you have to recognize you have a gift.

Two, you need to begin operating in your gift. Three, you have to seek God and ask Him where he wants you to apply your gift. From there, it's just a matter of Him illuminating each step you're supposed to be on," he says.

"That's where most of us are faltering, in the waiting. Joy comes in the morning, but some of us toss and turn so much through the night that the morning never gets to be the morning because we didn't go to sleep. You have to at least be willing to close your eyes and rest in the palm of His hands to embrace the morning.

"The greatest thing for me is that now, I get to sing every day. That is an amazing gift in itself, to do the thing I love to do. All I can say to anybody who loves to dream is thank God. Sometimes He pulls up in His Cadillac Seville and says, 'Jump in. You can ride.' I'm so glad He's driving, and I'm not. I don't know what our next destination is, but as passengers, we shouldn't even care. Just when he stops the car, get out and know what you're supposed to be doing. And never forget to push your dreams as if they are as light as a feather."

Gift Wrap

- When you recognize the weight of His favor, when you know how you are to use your gift, then you don't want to play around with it.

- It's very important to recognize that you cannot celebrate someone else until you celebrate yourself. And that ultimately means looking in the mirror daily and celebrating the river that's flowing in you. That's God.

- One, you have to recognize you have a gift. Two, you need to begin operating in your gift. Three, you have to seek God and ask Him where he wants you to apply your gift.

- The greatest thing for me is that now, I get to sing every day. That is an amazing gift in itself, to do the thing I love to do. All I can say to anybody who loves to dream is thank God. Sometimes He pulls up in His Cadillac Seville and says, 'Jump in. You can ride.'

Abraham's Other Gift: Faith

Appendix: Related Reading

Administration

1 Corinthians 12:28–31
Luke 14:28–30

Craftsmanship

Exodus 28:3–4
Exodus 31:1–11
Exodus 35:30–35

Discernment

1 Corinthians 12:7–11
1 John 4:1–6
1 Corinthians 2:9–16
2 Chronicles 2:12
Psalms 119:125
Proverbs 3:21
1 Kings 3:9
Hebrews 5:14

FAITH

1 Corinthians 12:7–11
Mark 5:25–34
Acts 27:21–25
Hebrews 11
Romans 4:18–21

GIVING

Romans 12:6–8
2 Corinthians 9:6–15
2 Corinthians 8:2–5
Mark 12:41–44
Matthew 6:3–4

KNOWLEDGE

And by knowledge shall the chambers be filled with all precious and pleasant riches.

—PROVERBS 24:4

For the transgression of a land many are the princes thereof, but by a man of understanding and knowledge the state thereof shall be prolonged.

—PROVERBS 28:2

For the LORD gives wisdom; from His mouth come knowledge and understanding.

—PROVERBS 2:6

The mind of the prudent acquires knowledge, And the ear of the wise seeks knowledge.

—PROVERBS 18:15

My people are destroyed for lack of knowledge: because thou hast rejected knowledge, I will also reject thee, that thou shalt be no priest to me: seeing thou hast forgotten the law of thy God, I will also forget thy children.

—HOSEA 4:6

WRITING

1 Tim. 3:14–15—As I write this letter to you, I hope to come and see you soon. But if I delay, this letter will let you know how we should conduct ourselves in God's household, which is the church of the living God, the pillar and support of the truth.

John 20:30–31—In his disciples' presence Jesus performed many other miracles which are not written down in this book. But these have been written in order that you may believe that Jesus is the Messiah, the Son of God, and that through your faith in him you may have life.

1 John 2:12–14—I write to you, my children, because your sins are forgiven for the sake of Christ. I write to you, fathers, because you know him who has existed from the beginning. I write to you, young men, because you have defeated the Evil One. I write to you, my children, because you know the Father. I write to you, fathers, because you know him who has existed from the beginning. I write

to you, young men, because you are string; the word of God lives in you, and you have defeated the Evil One.

Jude 1: 3—Dear friends, although I was very eager to write to you about the salvation we share, I felt compelled to write and urge you to contend for the faith that was once for all entrusted to God's holy people.

1 Timothy 3:14–15—Although I hope to come to you soon, I am writing you these instructions so that, if I am delayed, you will know how people ought to conduct themselves in God's household, which is the church of the living God, the pillar and foundation of the truth.

MUSIC

1 Samuel 16:14–23
1 Corinthians 14:26
Psalm 33:1–3
Psalm 96:1–2
Psalm 100:1–2
Psalm 149:3
Psalm 150:1–6
Colossians 3:16
2 Chronicles 5:12–13
2 Samuel 6:14–15

BIBLIOGRAPHY

The Gallup Organization *Building a Highly Engaged Workforce: How great managers inspire virtuoso performance.* Princeton, NJ: Gallup Poll 2002.

Adelaja, Sunday. *Money Won't Make Your Rich: God's Principles for True Wealth, Prosperity, and Success.* Kiev, Ukraine: Charisma House, 2009.

Blackaby, Henry. *Experiencing God: Knowing and Doing the Will of God.* Atlanta, GA: Broadman and Holman, 2008.

Foreman, George. *Knockout Entrepreneur: My Ten Count Strategy for Winning at Business.* Houston, TX: Thomas Nelson, 2009.

Barna, George. Survey Describes the Spiritual Gifts That Christians Say They Have. Ventura, California: Barna Group 2001.

THE MILESTONE BRAND

Free Gift Assessment: Learn Your Gift Today!

www.milestonebrand.com

7413 Six Forks Road

Suite 301

Raleigh, NC 27615

info@milestonebrand.com

ABOUT THE AUTHORS

Darrayl Miles is the Senior Vice President of The Milestone Brand, an insurance executive and a professional actor. Despite his hectic schedule, Darrayl aggressively finds time to enjoy his wife Twarnette. They have four children between them and reside in Central Florida.

Derrick Miles is the Chairman/CEO of The Milestone Brand and a corporate operations improvement consultant. He was a senior executive with operational responsibilities for several healthcare corporations prior to developing the Superhuman Performance® franchise. Derrick and his wife Michele have two children. They reside in the Triangle of North Carolina.